Environment and History

The taming of nature  and South Africa

William Beinart and Peter Coates

London and New York

First published 1995
by Routledge
11 New Fetter Lane, London EC4P 4EE

Simultaneously published in the USA and Canada
by Routledge
29 West 35th Street, New York, NY 10001

Typeset in Times by
Ponting–Green Publishing Services, Chesham, Bucks

Printed and bound in Great Britain by
T.J. Press (Padstow) Ltd, Padstow, Cornwall

British Library Cataloguing in Publication Data
A catalogue record for this book is available from the
British Library.

Library of Congress Cataloging in Publication Data
Beinart, William.
Environment and history: the taming of nature in the USA
    and South Africa / William Beinart and Peter Coates.
    p. cm. – (Historical connections)
    Includes bibliographical references and index.
    1. Man–Influence on nature–United States.
    2. Man–Influence on nature – South Africa.
    3. Environmentalism – United States – History.
    4. Environmentalism – South Africa–History.
    I. Coates, Peter. II. Title. III. Series.
    GF503.B45   1995
    333.9'13'0973–dc20   94–49712

ISBN 0–415–11468–3

Contents

Maps

Series editors' preface

Historical Connections is a series of short books on important historical topics and debates, written primarily for those studying and teaching history. The books will offer original and challenging works of synthesis that will make new themes accessible, or old themes accessible in new ways, build bridges between different chronological periods and different historical debates, and encourage comparative discussion in history.

If the study of history is to remain exciting and creative, then the tendency to fragmentation must be resisted. The inflexibility of older assumptions about the relationship between economic, social, cultural and political history has been exposed by recent historical writing, but the impression has sometimes been left that history is little more than a chapter of accidents. This series will insist on the importance of processes of historical change, and it will explore the connections within history: connections between different layers and forms of historical experience, as well as connections that resist the fragmentary consequences of new forms of specialism in historical research.

Historical Connections will put the search for these connections back at the top of the agenda by exploring new ways of uniting the different strands of historical experience, and by affirming the importance of studying change and movement in history.

Geoffrey Crossick
John Davis
Joanna Innes
Tom Scott

Preface

Green issues are pushing their way to the forefront of public interest and government policy throughout the developed and developing world. Many of these problems are conceived to be sudden new manifestations of human destructive capacity as we rush hellbent toward the end of the second millennium. Yet processes of environmental change are deeply rooted in the past. Perceptions of crisis, as well as attempts to confront them, are equally central, if neglected features of human history. An historical perspective on contemporary ecological dilemmas and responses is currently one of the most fascinating and relevant fields within the humanities and social sciences.

The emerging environmental history is especially accommodating to a comparative approach that can cut through political, geographical and disciplinary fences that enclose and isolate the interrelated materials of historical study. An exploration of the ecological impact of human economies and cultures is particularly rewarding in the worlds into which Europeans have swept over the past 500 years. This book is one of the first to test the transnational potential of an environmental approach to history within a comparative framework, provided in this instance by the United States and South Africa.

Environment and History has truly been a joint venture, nurtured by informal encounters that often tossed up uncanny similarities between our far-flung zones of expertise. Convergences of experience between the regions still resonate at the close of the project. Each chapter was thoroughly discussed before we both separately wrote drafts of three. The final result was the outcome of joint sessions in front of the blue screen. (The book was composed in a room with a view and we were able, as befits environmental historians, to refresh our spirits by watching the seasons at work on a birch and apple tree.) We can honestly say that most paragraphs – even sentences – bear the imprint of the styles and ideas of both of us. If the American examples sometimes seem a little more numerous, this simply reflects the far heavier volume of recent academic output on that country.

We would like to thank Graziella and Troth for their support in hectic times. We are also grateful to Jane Carruthers for her detailed comments on the manuscript.

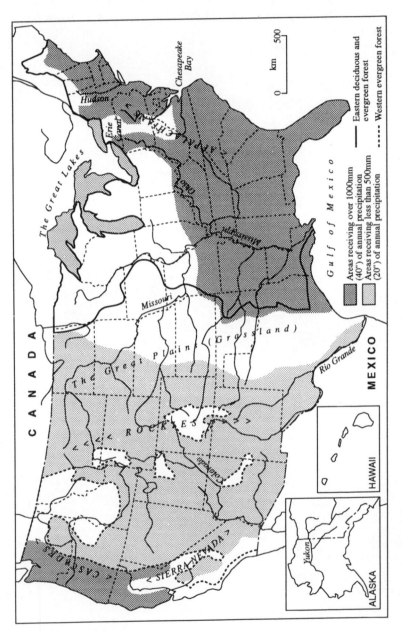

Map 1 Selected natural and topographical features of the United States

Areas receiving over 1000mm (40") of annual precipitation

Areas receiving less than 500mm (20") of annual precipitation

Eastern deciduous and evergreen forest

Western evergreen forest

CANADA

The Great Lakes

Hudson

Erie Canal

Chesapeake Bay

Gulf of Mexico

Missouri

The Great Plains (Grassland)

Rio Grande

ROCKIES

TAHOE

SIERRA NEVADA

CASCADES

MEXICO

km 500

HAWAII

ALASKA

Yukon

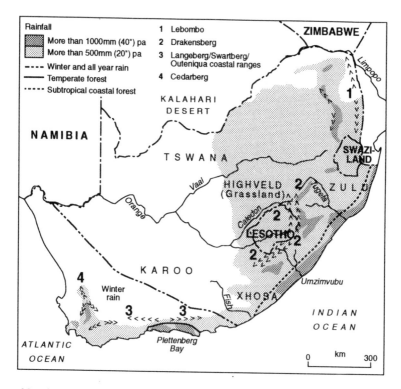

Rainfall

░ More than 1000mm (40") pa

▒ More than 500mm (20") pa

---- Winter and all year rain

—— Temperate forest

····· Subtropical coastal forest

1 Lebombo
2 Drakensberg
3 Langeberg/Swartberg/
  Outeniqua coastal ranges
4 Cedarberg

ZIMBABWE

NAMIBIA

KALAHARI
DESERT

TSWANA

Limpopo

SWAZI-
LAND

Vaal

HIGHVELD
(Grassland)

ZULU

Orange

Caledon

LESOTHO

Tugela

KAROO

Fish

XHOSA

Umzimvubu

4

Winter
rain

3

3

Plettenberg
Bay

ATLANTIC
OCEAN

INDIAN
OCEAN

0   km   300

Map 2 Selected natural and topographical features of South Africa

1 The nature of environmental history: the United States and South Africa compared

THE NATURE OF ENVIRONMENTAL HISTORY

Environmental history deals with the various dialogues over time between people and the rest of nature, focusing on reciprocal impacts. This fresh perspective, Clio's new greenhouse, recognizes that humans themselves are a part of, as well as apart from, nature. As Crosby insists, '[m]an is a biological entity before he is a Roman Catholic or a capitalist or anything else' (1972: xiii). Environmental history starts from a rather different assumption from most other branches of the discipline, which, whether concerned with high politics or forgotten folk, have tended to deal exclusively with intrahuman relations. In Cronon's words it is: 'a history which extends its boundaries beyond human institutions – economies, class and gender systems, political organizations, cultural rituals – to the natural ecosystems which provide the context for those institutions.' Such a history, he notes, 'inevitably brings to center stage a cast of nonhuman characters which usually occupy the margins of historical analysis if they are present in it at all' (1983: vii).

Though this recently generated sub-discipline is becoming a distinct field of study it has many precursors and antecedents – including historical geography, human ecology, frontier history, the 'total history' of the French *Annales* school and, less self-consciously, African history and anthropology. Environmental history has been most highly developed by Americans studying their own national experience. Initially, North American writers were mainly concerned with the despoliation of nature and the heroic rise of conservation. They were absorbed with the institutions and agencies of natural resource policy and protection, and with the great thinkers and actors such as Henry David Thoreau, John Muir and Aldo Leopold. It is no accident that this coincided with the rise of the modern environmental movement and the emergence of environmental issues as a major public concern in the 1960s and early 1970s. Environmental history in this form, however, was readily housed within established approaches of political, administrative and intellectual history.

While American historiography has been influential in the study of conservation in southern Africa, environmental historians of the former British empire show signs of rejecting this particular manifestation of 'Yankee imperialism'. Grove (1994) has investigated the long history of environmental concern occasioned by British expansion which, he suggests, predated the influential American book *Man and Nature* (1864) by George Perkins Marsh (see chapter 3). This points to the existence of a transnational and interconnected body of ideas and responses to comparable environmental situations.

Environmental history has in the meantime broadened out in other exciting directions, many of which deal with the history of the environment instead of the history of environmentalism. In our current, rather foreshortened view, fuelled by a powerful and angstful modern environmentalism, the destructive capacities of modern western society have come in for particular scrutiny. Some of the most striking environmental history, equating change with loss, explores facets of that destructiveness unleashed on a global scale by European expansion since the late fifteenth century. The treatment of environmental change as an underexplored aspect of colonialism is epitomized by Crosby who emphasizes the role of bio-ecological factors in the Europeanization of the world's temperate zones. Crosby assigns what he calls the 'biotic portmanteau' of plants, animals and diseases a leading role in the overall process of takeover.

As well as focusing on how whites (and their non-human allies) have mastered the natural world, scholars have become increasingly interested in how the vagaries of ecological interactions affect human societies. Crosby's work on ecological imperialism is also a call for the inclusion of the natural world in historical explanation. There are problems as well as challenges here for historians eager to pursue this kind of environmental history rather than content themselves with writing the history of a game reserve, national park or conservation luminary. Literally and figuratively, this requires an outdoor and open door orientation. Unravelling changes in the natural world itself demands the tools derived from training not only in history and the social sciences but also from natural sciences such as botany, zoology and ecology – a rounded view that might seem to call for more skills than even the average scientist possesses. Commanding these various specialisms may be a formidable task for any individual. But historians as generalists can achieve a sense of the central issues involved in discussing environmental change and continuity.

We should be able to offer some assessment of the nature and degree of ecological disturbance. A central informing concept of much recent environmental history has been degradation. Yet all human activity alters the composition of the natural world which in itself is never static. A critique which regards all change as decay begs the very question of the legitimacy of human survival, under whatever economic or ideological system. Distinguishing degradation, especially long-term, from change or transformation – less emotive terms – is rarely easy. The natural world has such a deep and elaborate human imprint that we must confront the awkward reality that we may search in vain for a recognizable and definable state of nature. Indeed, the very notion of a self-regulating, stable ecosystem may be more metaphysical than actual. Yet without a baseline, the attempt to characterize environmental change is that much harder.

Concepts of nature are always cultural statements. This may not strike Europeans as much of an insight, for Europe's landscape is so much of a blend. But in the new worlds – 'new' at least to Europeans – the distinction appeared much clearer not only to European settlers and visitors but also to their descendants. Hence the fond conceit of primeval nature untrammelled by human associations which could later find expression in a reverence for wilderness. Ecological relationships certainly have their own logic and in this sense 'nature' can be seen to have a self-regulating but not necessarily stable dynamic independent of human intervention. But the context for ecological interactions has increasingly been set by humanity. We may not determine how or what a lion eats but we certainly can regulate where the lion feeds.

Recent environmental history has not only been engaged in often anguished contemplation of modern environmental destructiveness. Preindustrial peoples have also received attention and the verdict on their environmental role has been far more ambivalent. There is a long tradition in western intellectual thought which sees pre-colonial people as living in some kind of harmony or balance with nature. This idea has taken different forms – disapproving as in the proverbial 'uncivilized and idle savage' who fails to capitalize on natural resource potential, and, especially with the recent embracing of green ideas, quite approving, even reverential. Much popular environmentalist literature today pictures pre-colonial communities, notably 'stone-age' Native Americans and the San[1] as 'children of nature'. They lived lightly upon the land, never achieving the technology or demographic weight to disrupt their environments.

Academic anthropology and ethnohistory are more critical of this image, casting indigenous peoples more as regulators. They were entirely capable of manipulating the natural world to their advantage, granted that their rituals, migrations and lifeways, consciously and otherwise, might have constrained the damaging effects of their behaviour. We should bear in mind that indigenous societies in North America were themselves once intruders encountering new worlds, having migrated from Asia over to Alaska 12,000 (and perhaps as many as 30,000) years ago, from where they fanned out down to Tierra del Fuego. Hunter-gatherer occupation of southern Africa dates back at least as long as this latter projection but the Bantu-speaking African[2] people moved across the subcontinent in a remarkably short space of time, colonizing southern Africa less than 2,000 years ago.

These extraordinary expansions must have been generated by growing population, opportunistic predation and local exhaustion of resources. Ancient settlers in the Americas, Australasia and elsewhere might have been at least partly responsible for the extermination, during the Pleistocene, of a number of the megafauna known from relatively recent archaeological records, either through overhunting or persistent burning of wide tracts of vegetation. Crosby paints these early migrants as aggressive colonizers in their own right. The 500th annniversary of Columbus's earth-shattering voyage was recently (1992) the occasion for condemnation as well as the usual celebration. Perhaps we should also have commemorated the anniversary of the crossing of the Bering land bridge.

Pre-contact aboriginal societies were certainly not 'people without history' immune from the processes of change (Wolf, 1982). Their capacity to coexist with nature has been questioned and they at least potentially faced crises of subsistence and destruction. Deforestation may have been a major factor in the collapse of Anasazi farming communities in the American southwest during the thirteenth century, a culture that had grown increasingly dependent on timber supplied from points up to fifty miles away through an elaborate tribute system that finally broke down.[3] Similarly, the fall of Great Zimbabwe (an ancient kingdom at the core of the modern-day nation) in the sixteenth century may have been the result of centuries of overgrazing around its heartland. Most likely, aboriginal relations with nature went through various stages: sustainable practices and ideas may represent the outcome of trial and error. Historical geographer Clarence Glacken (1967) has noted that while all societies create environmental 'problems', nevertheless elements within most have recognized the potential gravity of these impacts and some have debated means of containing disturbances.

In the older histories, the aboriginal 'victims' cease to play a role after the conquest. And many aborigines themselves, understandably, took the view that history 'ended' when whites gained the ascendancy. A more sophisticated history is looking at the ways in which the conquered adapted to new environments, technologies and cultural imports, trying to carve for themselves an active role. It is important to investigate what happened to these societies after contact with European trading networks from the sixteenth century in both the Americas and Africa. Disruption created opportunity for Plains Indians, for example, through the taming of feral mustangs. The mounted Sioux of folklore and films were thus a creation of colonial contact. In mountainous areas of South Africa, the Sotho adopted and bred their own ponies on which they then rode into battle with the Boers. In both America and Africa, horses and firearms enhanced hunting capacity across the racial divide. Whatever the aboriginal attitude to nature in the fifteenth century, new opportunities and markets may well have changed them by the eighteenth. The resurrection by the descendants of indigenous peoples of 'aboriginal' ideas about nature is a powerful ideological statement rather than good history. It has proved especially seductive for the disenchanted who seek inspiration in a precapitalist symbiosis of humankind and nature.

Capitalism did not trigger environmental change but most environmental historians of the colonial and post-colonial period, notably Worster and Cronon, lay great stress on the economic system of the dominant culture. To call it capitalist raises as many questions as it answers, in that capitalism itself metamorphosed over 500 years and continually created new demands and imperatives of exploitation.[4] Its insatiable demand for raw materials included the timbers of New England that replaced English oak as early as the seventeenth century as a source for British naval supplies. Plantation crops that fed and clothed the rising population of Europe demanded land as did the extensive ranching of sheep and cattle in Australasia, southern Africa and the Americas. Capitalism commoditized nature and redefined it according to new notions of value, giving communities the capacity to specialize, produce surpluses and function with greater independence from the local environment.

Rapidly changing technology, especially after late eighteenth-century industrialization, was an integral element of new economic systems and has provided a potent theme for environmental historians alert to the transformative capacities of capitalism. Not all technology was new. That most rudimentary of tools, fire, helped regulate the settler agrarian world as well as the hunting strategies of indigenous peoples (see chapters 2 and 3). Cronon comments that early visitors to New England were struck by the fact that though there were a large number of trees, the woods were 'remarkably open, almost parklike at times' (1983: 25). The setting of fires stimulated fresh growth which attracted game, a practice common to the Khoisan in Africa. Travellers through the settler grazing lands of the Orange Free State in the late nineteenth century also found mile upon mile of blackened stubble awaiting the rejuvenating spring rains.

But the enlisting of new European technology in the bid to transcend nature's restraints had a far larger impact. In both regions, hinterlands once considered worthless were reappraised in the light of technological advances such as steel ploughs and windmills (see chapter 4). Worster's *Rivers of Empire* (1985) illustrates how the harnessing of water through dams and irrigation canals enabled corporate agriculture to appropriate vast areas of the American West from the end of the nineteenth century. In stark refutation of the traditional notion of the frontier with its leitmotif of exuberant individualism and release from restraint, Worster postulates a hierarchical hydraulic society in which subjugation of nature and people are aspects of the same process.

The prowess of technology, whether in the form of fire or concrete irrigation channel, has in turn depended on scientific knowledge. Accordingly, the history of science has been bound up in complex if unsuspecting ways with environmental history, anticipating some of its concerns. Merchant (1980) regards Cartesian knowledge stemming from the scientific revolution of the seventeenth century as an essentially masculine system inseparable from the logic of environmental destruction, and examines the triumph over recent centuries of a patriarchal, mechanistic, deanimating, utilitarian attitude to nature.

In newly colonized worlds, the history of science is in part the investigation of how experts endeavoured to maximize exploitation of resources. Brockway's *Science and Colonial Expansion* (1979) examines the key role of botanical science as a means of distributing commercial crops around the British empire. Colonial botanical gardens were well established by the mid-seventeenth century; the Cape Town Gardens were just one example. In this way, tea reached India and Africa and the date palm and orange were transplanted to California. Within our comparative framework, we aim to provide a taste of the fruits of a ripening environmental history.

THE COMPARISON

In cherishing the particular in time and place, historians have tradition-
ally been less receptive to the comparative approach than geographers,
anthropologists and other social scientists. Comparative analyses of
North America and southern Africa, however, have a long history. The
central poles of comparison have been race relations and the frontier –
and there are intriguing parallels to explore. With regard to scholarly
production, much of the traffic has been one-way: American scholars
using southern Africa as a foil to examine their own experience.[5]

Race relations are of interest because both countries were the product
of colonial conquest and subjugation of indigenous peoples. Both settler
societies also imported slaves, though the institution in South Africa
never reached the scale and decisive role of slavery in the American
South. The combination of conquest and slavery gave rise to hierarchical racial systems. In the nineteenth century, there were moments
when a less rigid system seemed possible, only to recede in the face of
segregationist forces as the century drew to a close. Some of the most
stimulating comparative works (Fredrickson, 1981, 1988; Cell, 1982)
explore the cementing of white supremacy during this period.

Professional historians are not alone in finding the comparison
fruitful. For African intellectuals the American experience has also
been a fertile source of inspiration in addressing their own experience
of racial oppression. Some late-nineteenth-century African churches
had Afro-American origins while efforts at 'self-improvement' after the
Booker T. Washington model influenced black South African educational institutions (Jabavu, 1920). Garveyism, with its strong Pan-
African accent, intoxicated southern African urban radicals in the
1920s, as did the writings of black power ideologues such as Stokely
Carmichael fifty years later in the era of Steve Biko and the Soweto
uprising.

If race relations have commended themselves to black and white alike
as one cluster of comparative experience, frontier expansion furnishes
further historiographical crosscurrents. Southern Africa was the only
sub-Saharan part of the continent to undergo a major settler intrusion,
beginning in earnest in 1652 (after Portuguese precursors) – a half
century later than parallel events in North America. Much American
frontier history has suffered from an exaggerated sense of exceptional-
ism, yet beneath the benign and euphemistic veneer of 'settlement', the
American frontier struggle against indigenous people and natural world
was essentially no different from that of the white imperialist in
southern Africa. The European conquests of our regions were but two

aspects of the global expansion of capitalism whose tentacles fingered the globe's farthest recesses in the wake of Columbus and da Gama.

Eric Walker's analysis of the frontier tradition in South Africa (1930) explicitly borrowed from US historian Frederick Jackson Turner's environmentally deterministic idea (1893) of the raw frontier as an exhilarating formative experience and source of American national distinctiveness. Walker expressed a less optimistic view of the frontier tradition, seeing in it the roots of racial segregation. But both Walker and Turner were interested in the frontier's effect on settler society. More recent comparisons, most notably by Lamar and Thompson (1981), recognize the ethnocentricity of the frontier concept and concentrate less on settler character and more on conflict between intruders and indigenous peoples. Environmentally informed historians can take frontier analysis a step further by exploring human impact on the natural environment.

As with any comparison, there are limits beyond which it ceases to be useful (or possible) to show similarities. Moreover, by splicing together the two historical experiences, we do not intend to reduce the distinctiveness of either. This approach can also highlight differences, which are often just as illuminating. Two particular differences require emphasis, leaving aside the obvious contrasts in size of landmass and population.

In the first instance, the settler thrust in southern Africa was weaker, while the Americas were Europe's key frontier of expansion from 1492. Of the various new worlds opened up for European colonization in the temperate zones, the part of North America that became the USA (1783) was the primary destination for European emigrants, especially when emigration became a mass movement in the nineteenth century.

Second, North America's indigenes proved more vulnerable to incursion than Africans, who were not so isolated from other branches of humanity. While the Khoisan rapidly succumbed to disease, war and competition, the African people had sufficient immunity as well as economic and demographic weight to provide a check. Unlike the Khoisan and many Native American groups, the African chiefdoms had developed a more diversified, cultivating, pastoral and iron-using economy. The deeper the settlers intruded into the region, the more etiolated their influence. At the point, after the American Civil War (1861–5), that colonists were replacing the last more or less independent Native American remnants, so their South African counterparts were coming to terms with living with their numerically superior subjects. At the time when military conquest was completed in the 1880s (Gump, 1994), Native American numbers had reached their nadir of about a quarter of a million from a conservatively estimated high of 5 million in 1492. By contrast, black South African numbers (over 3 million at this time) do not seem to have dwindled and were beginning a significant rise.

As a result of these processes, North America has retained a decidedly different demographic profile which confirmed white hegemony and undergirded their economic and political power. In this respect, the United States is a prime example of what Crosby (1986) calls 'lands of demographic takeover', such as Australia, New Zealand, Canada and Argentina. South Africa entered the twentieth century with only 20 per cent of its 5 million population classified as 'white'. Conversely, American whites comprised almost 90 per cent of its 100 million. In the United States, 10 per cent were descended from black slaves. A comparable percentage of South Africans were also at least partly descended from imported labour, namely, slaves and nineteenth-century Asian indentured workers. Whereas indigenous black South Africans made up nearly 70 per cent of the total population, however, Native Americans were barely a third of 1 per cent.

THE FRONTIER ENVIRONMENT

As we have argued, historians of the United States and to a lesser extent of South Africa are rediscovering the environmental dimensions of conquest. To our knowledge, there has been little attempt to explore comparatively this inescapably central element. History, at its most fundamental level, records not only human interactions but the incorporation of the natural world into the human world. These themes are especially germane and potent during the rapid social and economic transformations involved in colonization. The availability of natural resources, animate and inanimate, did much to determine the pattern and character of our regions' histories. Settlers' location on the margins of expanding commercial empires accelerated the conversion of nature's store into commodities.

For native flora and fauna, indigenous people and settlers alike, water was the critical resource shaping the possibilities for existence. In southern Africa, precipitation declines (unevenly) westward from the east coast and northward from the south. In pre-colonial southern Africa, well over half the indigenous population lived in the narrow belt of warm and well-watered land on the east coast in the shadow of the Drakensberg – less than a quarter of the total area of the country – in contrast to the sparsely inhabited western expanses. Similarly, ample rainfall and a temperate climate dictated that the east coast of North

America (sectioned off by the Appalachian ranges) was most heavily populated, and had the most elaborate agrarian economies – indigenous and settler. It is often forgotten that much of the western two-thirds of the continental United States (as roughly the same proportion of South Africa) is arid (below 10 inches of precipitation) or semi-arid (less than 20 inches).

In southern and central Africa, patterns of settlement and occupation were deeply affected by disease. Malaria was never a total obstacle and Africans coexisted with the disease over many centuries, but before quinine and other drugs came into general use its presence discouraged settler occupation in areas where it was rife. Trypanosomiasis, a parasite carried by the tsetse fly, which caused sleeping sickness in humans and was also devastating for cattle and horses, inhibited white intrusion. The map of European settlement in southern Africa tends to coincide with less disease-ridden locales.

There were no comparable 'no go' zones in North America, though the malignant forms of malaria, yellow fever and hookworm were brought to the southern colonies with African slaves. These sub-tropical diseases that flourished in the Chesapeake made heavy inroads into the initial settler generations (Cowdrey, 1983: 26–8, 36–9). Indeed, alleged African resistance to disease was a major factor in the shift from white servitude to black slavery as the preferred labour system. In the longer term, however, diseases, virtually all of which were imported, worked almost entirely in the interests of the intruders. Their quite staggering consequences are epitomized by the scourge of smallpox, one of the most lethal of the so-called 'virgin soil epidemics'. While guarding against an overly deterministic approach, we should acknowledge that new ills go a considerable way to explain the relative ease and extent of the European takeover. As one ethnohistorian (Jennings, 1975) has suggested, 'widowed land' is a more accurate characterization of North America during the settlement phase than the customary 'virgin land'.

In both regions, indigenous populations were unevenly displaced or incorporated. Whereas groups like the Khoisan had lost their independence, and most even their language, by the mid-nineteenth century, some large African chiefdoms of the interior had hardly yet encountered the colonial presence. The scale of displacement and dispossession was greater and its pace more rapid in North America. Yet even there, Native American communities occupying the interior grasslands, while dealing with whites, could survive into the second half of the nineteenth century. In the far north of Canada and Alaska, smaller groups of predominantly hunter-gatherers who occupied terrain of marginal value to agrarian settlers retained their autonomy for longer and have not suffered any comparable erosion of their land base. In similar fashion, the San of the Kalahari desert interacted with the modern economy, yet in ways that sustained their cultural survival on the desert margins.

In addition, indigenous people regrouped and reasserted themselves as new chiefdoms emerged in the eighteenth and nineteenth centuries, empowered not least by acquisition of European trade items. In South Africa, the early colonial phase coincided with a period of centralization producing new nodes of power in the nineteenth century and inclusive identities such as the Sotho on the highveld and the Zulu on the east coast. Zulu expansion involved forcible absorption of surrounding communities. Nor was the horse-powered westward expansion of the Sioux on to the Great Plains, like the later and better known white version, an occupation of empty space; it occurred at the expense of resident tribes. All of this jostling for territory and control involved considerable interchange of knowledge and lifeways. In particular, indigenous peoples taught settlers how to cope with their exotic environments; specifically, the location of water and game and how to hunt and fish. Recent American literature (Kupperman, 1980; White, 1991a; Faragher, 1992) marks a shift away from preoccupation with primarily antagonistic relationships to the exploration of areas of accommodation. On the earlier frontier, before significant capital had been introduced, some settlers 'went native' or were perceived to do so. The American frontier, in Turner's phrase, 'strips off the garments of civilization and arrays him in the hunting shirt and the moccasin. It puts him in the log cabin of the Cherokee . . . and runs an Indian palisade around him. Before long he has gone to planting Indian corn' (Turner, 1893: 4). The French Catholic trappers of the northern woods *(coureurs de bois)* were a case in point, taking Native partners, who often functioned as key intermediaries (Van Kirk, 1983). The South African 'trekboer' (mobile pastoral farmer) adopted the indigenous fat-tailed, hairy sheep as a primary resource. With his musket and *velskoen* (animal hide shoes), he was viewed as semi-barbarized by visiting Europeans. The trekboers grew maize and loved their American tobacco, like their Dutch forebears in Europe (Schama, 1987). Both crops had already been adapted by Africans to the local environment.

All frontiers had phases, partly determined by the nature of local resources, partly by patterns of growth and demand for raw materials in Europe and colonial sub-metropoles. Sometimes they followed each other in rapid succession, in turn reshaping the natural environment. Though there is no simple sequence, hunting and trapping were often in the vanguard. The search for sub-soil wealth such as silver and diamonds could draw large numbers of people into otherwise unsettled regions and create urban enclaves like Denver and Kimberley from which new resource demands radiated outwards. The frontier 'closed' with the transition to intensive agriculture and barbed wire fences.

North America, contrary to the dominant Anglocentric conception of a singular east–west sweep across the continent, was penetrated by a four-pronged movement, three of them initiated in the early seventeenth century. French trappers moved down the St Lawrence and through the Great Lakes into the Mississippi valley. The Spanish pressed up from Mexico into the southwest behind an essentially pastoral frontier, and in the process transformed Native American economies so that horses, sheep and goats were grazing parts of the interior west long before the first transcontinental railroads. The Russian presence on the west coast, spanning coastal waters from Alaska down to northern California, left less of an impression – their major interest being the harvesting of marine mammal furs. But the fourth, best known, agrarian settler dimension of this multi-faceted and pan-European invasion, emanating primarily from the British Isles and swelling into the famous westward movement, was the prevailing force that finally produced the United States.

Southern Africa was pierced by a tri-pronged assault. The Portuguese, based on the Mozambican coast, established ports in the sixteenth and seventeenth centuries. They took armies into the interior of the Zimbabwean highveld in search of gold and slaves, much as the first Spanish conquistadores had infiltrated the interior of North America as far north as what is now Kansas. The Portuguese were repulsed by the end of the seventeenth century, but had they succeeded in conquering this area, South Africa may have been colonized from the north rather than from the south. Cape Town originated, as did Manhattan (New Amsterdam) and the Bronx, as a Dutch outpost: like New York City's Harlem (Nieuw Haarlem), its older streets and suburbs bear Dutch names (Oranjezicht and Tamboerskloof).

Dutch hunters and trekboers dispersed from a settled agrarian society in their ox wagons to become the major agents of settler expansion in the eighteenth and nineteenth centuries. Moving generally from southwest to northeast, their further flung sorties into the northern Transvaal were determined largely by lust for ivory. From the Cape to the northern Transvaal was a distance roughly equivalent to that between the Appalachian crest and the eastern margins of the sub-humid trans-Mississippi West. Ultimately, as in North America (1664), but later (1806), this other 'new netherland' succumbed to superior British colonial competition which consolidated the commercialization of the subcontinent and increasingly gave it a unity.

Intruding settlers to some degree always looked back to the sea, to the market economies from which they had come. Their metropolitan orientations meant that while they could sometimes adopt native garb, they could not reproduce the same subsistence-oriented way of life. At the same time, those largely self-contained economies were being reduced to satellites orbiting within an expanding European universe. In general, local markets were far more restricted in South Africa and its economy remained more colonial. The relative absence of urban markets meant there was limited opportunity for capitalism to develop before the discovery of diamonds and gold in the 1860s–1880s. The American colonies, before and after independence, proved much more attractive to outside investment. By the early twentieth century, the United States had become exceptional internationally in its self-sufficiency. In the twentieth-century corporate industrial era the scale of growth in the USA had become so much greater that the comparative method has strict limitations. By the 1920s, the majority of Americans were classified as urban dwellers, a watershed not reached in South Africa until the 1980s.

To conclude, environmental history lends itself to a comparative approach that transcends the boundaries of history written from the standpoint of the state or nation. This more natural history is a fecund source of interaction and sharp point of intersection between history and the sciences, both social and natural. We are particularly interested in human relations with other creatures – wild and tame – and with trees, grasslands and agriculture. The built or urban environment is a more muted theme, featuring chiefly as a source of pressure upon rural environments.[6]

We hope to balance discussion of political economy and ecological change, illustrating their interaction. Human attitudes to nature, especially responses to perceived environmental degradation, including the diagnosis of problems and formulation of solutions, recur as an organizing thread and receive particular weight in the final chapter. For it is people who initiate history, even environmental history, and people – sometimes actual individuals – remain our focus regardless of the supporting cast we have assembled. While we are alert to pre-colonial change wrought by aboriginal practices, the bulk of our attention is devoted to the period between the mid-nineteenth and mid-twentieth centuries, when the transformation of the physical environment accelerated on a global scale and modern ideas of conservation and environmentalism took root.

NOTES

1 The original hunter–gatherer communities established for thousands of years in southern Africa and partly displaced by African expansion.
2 We use the term 'African' to denote the indigenous peoples of the region who lived in established political systems when encountered by whites. In North America, the term 'Red Indian' has been emphatically abandoned and replaced by the more sensitive label 'Native American' (invariably capitalized to avoid confusion with native-born whites) but the appellation 'American Indian' remains respectable in academic discourse if not in activist circles. In South Africa, however, the term 'native' was adopted by settlers and became coated with their racial ideas. It has long been rejected by indigenous people in favour of 'African' or 'black'.
3 Proof that now treeless desert was once forested comes from pine needles preserved in the solidified urine of the pack rat taken from their fossilized nests.
4 Exploitation, a central Marxist concept with reference to the abuse of human labour, is a recurring theme in environmental history. It usually features as a synonym for abuse of nature but can simply denote use.
5 This book concentrates largely on the political units that became the USA and South Africa, but makes frequent reference to other parts of the North American and southern African regions.
6 Our focus is firmly terrestrial; space constraints cause us to omit coastal waters, their lifeforms, and topics such as marine pollution.

REFERENCES AND FURTHER READING

Environmental history

Anderson, David and Grove, Richard (eds) (1987) *Conservation in Africa: People, Policies and Practice*, Cambridge: Cambridge University Press.
Beinart, William (ed.) (1989) 'The politics of conservation in Southern Africa', Special Issue, *Journal of Southern Africa Studies*, 15 (2), 143–392.
Brockway, Lucile (1979) *Science and Colonial Expansion: The Role of the British Royal Botanic Garden*, New York: Academic Press.
Coates, Peter (1994) 'Chances with wolves: renaturing western history', *Journal of American Studies*, 28 (August), 241–54.
Cowdrey, Albert (1983) *This Land, This South: An Environmental History*, Lexington: University Press of Kentucky.
Cronon, William (1983) *Changes in the Land: Indians, Colonists, and the Ecology of New England*, New York: Hill & Wang.
Crosby, Alfred (1972) *The Columbian Exchange: Biological and Cultural Consequences of 1492*, Westport: Greenwood Press.
—— (1986) *Ecological Imperialism: The Biological Expansion of Europe, 900 to 1900*, New York: Cambridge University Press.
Glacken, Clarence (1967) *Traces on the Rhodian Shore: Nature and Culture in Western Thought from Ancient Times to the End of the Eighteenth Century*, Berkeley: University of California Press.

Grove, Richard (1990) 'The origins of environmentalism', *Nature*, 345 (3 May), 11–14.

—— (1994) *Green Imperialism*, Cambridge: Cambridge University Press.

Jacobs, Wilbur R. (1980) 'Indians as ecologists and other environmental themes in American frontier history', in Christopher Vecsey and Robert W. Venables (eds), *American Indian Environments: Ecological Issues in Native American History*, Syracuse: Syracuse University Press.

Merchant, Carolyn (1980) *The Death of Nature: Women, Ecology and the Scientific Revolution*, San Francisco: Harper & Row.

—— (ed.) (1993) *Major Problems in American Environmental History*, Lexington: D.C. Heath.

Nash, Roderick (1970) 'The state of environmental history', in Herbert J. Bass (ed.) *The State of American History*, Chicago: Quadrangle.

Petulla, Joseph M. (1977) *American Environmental History: The Exploitation and Conservation of Natural Resources*, San Francisco: Boyd & Fraser.

Pyne, Stephen J. (1982) *Fire in America: A Cultural History of Wildland and Rural Fire*, Princeton: Princeton University Press.

Simmons, I.G. (1993) *Environmental History: A Concise Introduction*, Oxford: Blackwell.

White, Richard (1985) 'American environmental history: the development of a new historical field', *Pacific Historical Review*, 54, 297–335.

Worster, Donald (1985) *Rivers of Empire: Water, Aridity and the Growth of the American West*, New York: Pantheon.

—— (ed.) (1989) *The Ends of the Earth: Perspectives on Modern Environmental History*, New York: Cambridge University Press.

General

Wolf, Eric (1982) *Europe and the People Without History*, Berkeley: University of California Press.

Southern Africa

Beinart, William (1994) *Twentieth-Century South Africa*, Oxford: Oxford University Press.

Davenport, T.R.H. (1991) *South Africa: A Modern History*, London: Macmillan.

Elphick, R. (1977) *Kraal and Castle: Khoikhoi and the Founding of White South Africa*, New Haven: Yale University Press.

Elphick, R. and Giliomee, H. (eds) (1989) *The Shaping of South African Society, 1652–1840*, Cape Town: Maskew Miller Longman.

Marks, Shula and Atmore, A. (eds) (1980) *Economy and Society in Pre-Industrial South Africa*, London: Longman.

Maylam, P. (1986) *A History of the African People of South Africa*, Cape Town: David Philip.

Schama, Simon (1987) *The Embarrassment of Riches: An Interpretation of Dutch Culture in the Golden Age*, London: Collins.

Thompson, Leonard (1990) *A History of South Africa*, New Haven: Yale University Press.

United States

Faragher, John Mack (1992) *Daniel Boone: The Life and Legend of an American Pioneer*, New York: Henry Holt.

Jennings, Francis (1975) *The Invasion of America: Indians, Colonialism, and the Cant of Conquest*, New York: Norton.

Kupperman, Karen O. (1980) *Settling with the Indians: The Meeting of English and Indian Cultures in America, 1580–1640*, London: J.M. Dent.

Meinig, Donald W. (1986) (1993) *The Shaping of America: A Geographical Perspective on 500 Years of History*; vol. 1, *Atlantic America, 1492–1800*; vol. 2, *Continental America, 1800–1867*, New Haven: Yale University Press.

Turner, Frederick Jackson (1893) 'The significance of the frontier in American history' in F.J. Turner (1920) *The Frontier in American History*, New York: Henry Holt.

Van Kirk, Sylvia (1983) *'Many Tender Ties': Women in Fur Trade Society in Western Canada, 1670–1870*, Norman: University of Oklahoma Press.

White, Richard (1983) *The Roots of Dependency: Subsistence, Environment and Social Change Among the Choctaws, Pawnees, and Navajos*, Lincoln: University of Nebraska Press.

—— (1991a) *The Middle Ground: Indians, Empires and Republics in the Great Lakes Region, 1650–1815*, New York: Cambridge University Press.

—— (1991b) *'It's Your Misfortune and None of My Own': A New History of the American West*, Norman: University of Oklahoma Press.

Comparative

Cell, John (1982) *The Highest Stage of White Supremacy: The Origins of Segregation in South Africa and the American South*, New York: Cambridge University Press.

Fredrickson, George (1981) *White Supremacy: A Comparative Study of American and South African History*, New York: Oxford University Press.

—— (1988) *The Arrogance of Race: Historical Perspectives on Slavery, Racism and Social Inequality*, Middletown: Wesleyan University Press.

Gump, James (1994) *The Dust Rose Like Smoke: The Subjugation of the Zulu and Sioux*, Lincoln: University of Nebraska Press.

Jabavu, D.D.T. (1920) *The Black Problem*, Lovedale: Lovedale Institution Press.

Lamar, Howard and Thompson, Leonard (eds) (1981) *The Frontier in History: North America and Southern Africa Compared*, New Haven: Yale University Press.

Walker, Eric (1930) *The Frontier Tradition in South Africa*, Oxford: Oxford University Press.

2 Hunting and animals: from game to wildlife

The hunt was a seminal rite of passage for young Boers at the Cape, Scots-Irish farmboys in Appalachia, San Bushmen and Sioux alike; a ceremony of initiation into the larger community and an instrument of social cohesion for both indigenous peoples and settlers. The significance of hunting as a means of survival in pre-colonial and early colonial societies, hitherto largely underexplored, is becoming recognized by historians. The role of hunting products in the early international market economies has also caught their attention. Material relating to the killing of wild animals is increasingly valued as a lucrative point of entry into environmental history, particularly regarding male relations with nature.

Our major concern in this chapter lies with hunting as an agent of environmental change, in which it is often assigned a critical role. Hunting has been men's (as distinct from women's) essential activity for the bulk of human evolution. But to speak of hunting as an undifferentiated enterprise is about as useful analytically as a blunt spear. We need to distinguish types of hunter and phases of hunting: pre-colonial and colonial era indigenous hunting; settler hunting for subsistence and trade; hunting as an adjunct to agriculture or a subsidy for other frontier enterprises; and élite hunting for the thrill of the chase, commonly called sport in the nineteenth and early twentieth centuries. In the aftermath of the predatory nineteenth century, when the killing reached its zenith, a reaction of sorts began to set in as some of the human raptors changed their spots. We conclude by attempting to explain this hesitant transition as expressed by tighter hunting controls, early game reserves and wildlife refuges.

PRE-COLONIAL HUNTING

The first American hunting frontier probably opened as soon as Asians trekked over, probably in pursuit of migratory herds, and swept down to the tip of Patagonia in what is now thought to be a fairly rapid movement; one palaeoecologist estimates a rate of ten miles a year. San hunters inhabited South Africa at least 30,000 years ago. Heavy dependence on hunting for meat dictated a mobile and adaptable mode of life to follow the migratory herds. But hunting, at least in historic times, did not only involve the killing of animals where they happened to be found. Aboriginal subsistence needs dictated extensive 'outdoor housekeeping'. Regular burning can increase the nutritional quality of browse for grazers, setting in train a process of floral succession that attracts game and allows numbers to increase. Abundant game was therefore sometimes a sign that vegetation had been manipulated. Burning also improved visibility and access for hunters. The California coastal range's characteristic landscape of chaparral (open evergreen oak and manzanita forest) was a product of Indian fire management. Some also argue for a central aboriginal role in producing the ostensibly 'natural' environment of the Plains grassland. When anthropologist Richard Lee studied the Kalahari San people in the 1950s and 1960s he found extensive use of fire – which sometimes ran out of control – even in that semi-arid environment. Botanists in the western Cape have found that the reproduction of some of the extraordinary variety of fynbos species, a unique fine-leafed shrub and bush mix including proteas, is facilitated by fire – both natural and set. (Frequent fires, however, can destroy their reproductive cycle and favour similarly adapted Australian invaders.)

Though African (as distinct from San) societies were more agrarian than their North American counterparts, hunting was a part of all African life. A major difference between Africans and Native Americans was the general absence of domestic animals in the latter's pre-contact economies – the only real exception being the use of the dog travois (sledge) on the Plains. Accordingly, in Africa, hunting was essential not only for food but to protect livestock from both feline and canine predators. In the 1830s, Captain William Cornwallis Harris, author of a famous early hunting saga, had been driven inland from the Cape by the paucity of game. Visiting the royal homestead of the Ndebele king, he found it 'strewed with the bones of wild animals' – not least the skulls of lions, which paid the price for preying on cattle (Beinart, 1990: 163). When Africans adopted woolled sheep in the nineteenth century, jackals which fed on the growing flocks became seen as a curse. The Tswana stepped up their hunting and chiefs found a use for the striped pelts in the manufacture of coats and hats. North American Indian adoption of European livestock was more limited, though when the Navajo became pastoralized in the sixteenth century predators were similarly redefined as undesirable neighbours.

Most commentators have stressed the sustainability of aboriginal hunter-gatherer practices before colonial contact. By sustainable they mean the ecological viability over the long run of economic practices. It is often suggested that Native Americans and San hunted with restraint, killing frugally what they needed to survive. Anthropologists of the San documented in great detail the careful use of gut for bowstrings, ostrich shells for water and hide for penis sheaths. Aboriginal ideological systems are often highlighted in explanations of the sustainability of pre-colonial societies. A cherished fable about the desert San concerns their belief that a neighbouring band whom they respected resembled gemsbok. When out hunting they took great pains not to harm these people. 'If a group of gemsbok people are out grazing and notice that a Bushman hunter is drawing his bow at them, they will say to him: "do not shoot us, we are not gemsbok," and the hunter will naturally leave them alone' (Thomas, 1958: 147).

Similarly, every account of Sioux culture at its nineteenth-century height lists the multifarious uses for each bit of buffalo, including shoulder blades for hoes, back fat for hair grease, and tongues (which were very rough) for hair brushes. A Gary Larson 'The Far Side' cartoon depicts an Indian holding up an odd-shaped piece of buffalo, explaining to a crowd that while he does not know what it is he knows that it's the only part they do not use. But it is worth noting, particularly in connection with wildlife depletion, that not all aboriginal magico-religious beliefs encouraged what we could now call conservation consciousness. Many American indigenes believed animal numbers were supernaturally determined and thus had little appreciation of the role of human agency.

Regardless of the practical impact of these beliefs, an intricate symbolic-totemic world was constructed around pre-colonial hunting. Chiefs and other notables wore animal product insignia, such as ivory bangles, to convey their positions. Elaborate, days-long performances like the Sioux sun dance, designed to evoke the spirits on behalf of good hunting, in which the hunter became the hunted, dominated the ceremonial world of the Plains Indians. The quiver was the San symbol of manhood. For African leaders, control over hunting for the distribution of meat, and particularly trade in ivory, were mechanisms for asserting power, stamping territorial authority and defining gender roles. There is little evidence of female hunting, at least not of larger animals. Women and children were, however, engaged in guarding crops and scaring animals away. Though the nineteenth-century romantic artist

Alfred Jacob Miller depicted Indian women hunting buffalo, they generally came into their own during the processing stages of skinning, cooking and manufacturing. As the Plains tribes extended their hunting capacity and range on the back of the horse, so the more female sphere of agriculture shrank and with it a measure of women's influence was eroded.

Those uncomfortable with the latest repackaging of the myth of the noble savage into the notion of indigenous person as the first ecologist, stress the role of aboriginal overhunting in wildlife depletion – even during pre-colonial times. The journals of the Lewis and Clark expedition of 1804–6, sent to explore the recently purchased territory that extended national boundaries to the Pacific, contain information about Native American buffalo jumps; entire herds were funnelled over cliffs, observations lately confirmed by archaeological evidence in the form of bones at kill sites and piles of stones that secured the edges of hunters' tents. A mid-nineteenth-century traveller in southern Africa, Francis Galton, a close relative of Charles Darwin, found Khoisan peoples driving large quantities of game into pitfalls (Wilson and Thompson, 1969: 48). Some of the surplus meat was dried but it is unlikely that all the kill was consumed.

We must be careful with such evidence because blaming aboriginals for wildlife losses is a tradition that runs deep into settler thinking. European disapproval of 'wanton' Indian hunting methods in North America was matched by settler condemnation of African trap and pitfall methods as wasteful and cruel. It seems that indigenes were locked in a no-win situation in terms of how Europeans viewed their husbandry of natural resources; by contrast to the accusation of overuse of game, their underuse of resources was cited by whites as justification for taking over 'vacant' lands for cultivation.

SETTLER HUNTING

The speed and intensity of settlement in North America suggests that natural resources were more abundant on the American frontier than in southern Africa. While true of valuable farmlands and timber, when it came to wildlife North America was certainly overshadowed by the variety of southern African species. In particular, the latter region hosted a larger range of predators. Southern Africa, De Kiewiet also boasted (1941: 11), was 'the richest game country the world had ever known'. This may have been a valid claim regarding the diversity of large herbivores but North America was better endowed with fur-bearers.

The desire for wildlife products was a leading motive for frontier penetration by expectant capitalists (often misportrayed as refugees from civilization) in the vanguard of an international economy. European and Asian demand for skins, furs and ivory (often determined by consumer whim) grafted a new monetary value on to products of the hunt which had been absent in pre-colonial times. Like the elephant hunters of southern Africa who penetrated deep into the interior in advance of settlement, the white and *métis* Rocky Mountain fur trapper of the early nineteenth century guided westward expansion. American corporate capitalism grew up with the fur trade, John Jacob Astor's American Fur Company (founded 1808) being the largest US firm of its day. In similar style, ivory dominated the Transvaal's export economy for three decades before minerals were exploited. Market hunting was a way for aspiring landowners (often sons of farmers) to acquire the means to set themselves up – especially since fertile, well-watered, accessible farmland was at more of a premium than in the United States.

The elephant was butchered not least to provide items like knife handles and billiard balls. The American market predominated by the early twentieth century, until plastics took over in the 1940s. Rhino horns provided Middle Eastern dagger handles or, ground into powder, were consumed as cure-alls in the Orient. The decision of Parisian milliners to switch to silk in the 1830s and 1840s offered a last-minute reprieve for the embattled North American beaver that ensured its survival long before conservationists were active on behalf of wildlife protection. The vogue in ostrich feather hats and flamboyant boa scarves, daringly named after the South American constricting snake, transformed a wild bird, through breeding, into a farmed animal. American buffalo tongues were sometimes the only part of the animal removed. Smoked, it was a delicacy in European restaurants and a perusal of Victorian cookbooks will remind us of the elevated status of game meats at that time.

Indigenous hunting became enmeshed in this white colonial net and changed radically in the process. European reliance on indigenous knowledge meant Alaskan Aleuts were coerced into massive slaughter of otters by Russian *promyshlenniki* (fur traders) who took their families hostage. San hunters were renowned in life as well as literature for their tracking genius – one of the few areas in which superior native skill was acknowledged. African client hunters, the *swart skuts*, breached the malarial and tsetse belts in the 1860s when their Boer masters held back for fear of disease.

By the mid-seventeenth century, Indians engaged in the fur trade had virtually wiped out New England's beaver. Indians also supplied buffalo robes in the nineteenth-century trans-Mississippi West.[1] In return for animal products, stone age peoples – already in the habit of elaborate trade and barter – acquired the benefits of the iron and textile age – as well as whiskey, tobacco, beads, coffee, sugar and hand mirrors. Indian market hunting probably contributed to the demise of the buffalo in its last stronghold on the Plains. Flores argues (1991), using biological and anthropological data to reconstruct numbers, that the lurid, better-documented holocaust of the 1870s was really just the 'shaggy's' *coup de grâce*. In addition, buffalo grazing was threatened on the Southern Plains in the early nineteenth century by some quarter to a half million domesticated horses, plus two million mustangs. Drought and introduced cattle diseases also contributed to the decline.

While there are examples of coercion, the extent to which indigenous peoples were willing participants remains a vital issue. For some, trade goods and enhanced killing capacity were sufficient to undermine sustainable practices. But historians have also argued that this seemingly shortsighted rapacity can only be properly explained by reference to the entire traumatic package of almost seismic disruptions inflicted by disease, territorial encroachment, Christianity and, not least, alcohol.

Ultimately, however, the buffalo's fate, like the elephant's, was sealed by the direct action of white hunters. In the 1870s German tanners found a way to convert soft buffalo hides into cheap and durable leather. The British army, marching across the globe in much the same way as the buffalo had once roamed North America, proved a particularly good customer. A government survey in 1894 could find only 85 wild buffalo, with another 1,000 or so in parks or on ranches as curios. Similarly, but a little earlier, there were probably only a few hundred elephants left within the boundaries of South Africa, secreted in the far north or the dense bush of the Addo in the eastern Cape. Had the elephant's range, by chance, been restricted to South Africa, it too would have teetered on the brink of extinction.

Accounts of the extinction of fabled species such as the passenger pigeon, blaaubok (blue antelope), and quagga (a less-striped type of zebra) are staples of the literature on environmental change. And two of the best-known personalities in American history are Martha, the last passenger pigeon, and Incas, the last Carolina parakeet, who died in the Cincinnati zoo in 1914 and 1918 respectively. Perhaps less well known is the last quagga that died in Amsterdam zoo in 1883 (Skead, 1980: 369).

The killing of wildlife also featured in connection with various other white needs, among them, given the uncertainty of arable production, the need to eat. For the majority of the first settler generation in both our regions, wild animals were primarily a food supply – conserving, not least, their own precious livestock. Involuntary African migrants to North America also valued wild meat. Generally barred from owning guns, slaves deployed a variety of methods to supplement their protein-deficient diets, illustrated by Joel Chandler Harris's Uncle Remus stories of the late nineteenth century. Snares, deadfalls, nets and stakes secured rabbit, squirrel, opossum, raccoon and the occasional deer.

Hunting was regarded as a fundamental settler right, key tenet of a more egalitarian frontier society. Laws defined game as common property which permitted, though sometimes at the cost of trespass, its free taking. On the frontier in South Africa, the *jagtersgemeenskap* (hunting fellowship) potently socialized Boer youth. One member of the antebellum plantocracy of the American South commented that rigid restrictions on hunting in Britain seemed to be 'the sorest and best remembered of [the] griefs' forcing emigration (William Elliott, as quoted in Marks, 1993: 33). As such it proved very hard to convict poachers. Visiting British hunters and settlers, in like style, celebrated the freedom of the kill and lack of social constraint in Africa.

Unsurprisingly, hunter-heroes loom large in the white mythology and literature of both regions. America's first homespun literary celebrity, Leatherstocking (alias Natty Bumppo/Hawkeye), who made the first of five appearances in James Fenimore Cooper's *The Pioneers* (1823), was modelled on the already legendary backwoodsman Daniel Boone. Rider Haggard spent some time in the Transvaal in the 1870s and had first-hand experience from which to conjure up the prototypical white elephant hunter, Allan Quatermain in *King Solomon's Mines* (1885). Legendary politicians such as Paul Kruger, the last president of the independent republic of the Transvaal and for whom one of Africa's largest and best-known national parks was named, reputedly came to attention as an elephant slayer, while folklore has him killing a lion in barehanded combat. Davy Crockett, the 'Coonskin congressman' from Tennessee (who recalled that garnering votes was just like racking up skins), was catapulted into the political arena by his reputation as an indefatigable bear hunter. The pages of nineteenth-century British imperial literature trumpeted hunting's value as a training ground for soldiers, a handy transferable skill in the empire-building enterprise.

Whereas the first generation of white hunter–farmers, like their aboriginal predecessors, relied on game for subsistence, the more settled agrarian communities that superseded them had less use for wildlife in any respect. Intellectual historians have highlighted the moral good wrought by taming the landscape and eradicating its wildness. Livestock predators such as jackals, hyenas, wild dogs, the large cats, coyotes, wolves, eagles, cougar and grizzly bear were classified as vermin (varmints in North America and *ongedierte* – non-animal – in Afrikaans) and became their *bêtes noires*. Shooting, poisoning and trapping were part of the rhythms of farm life but these outlaws were rarely taken for meat. As early as the seventeenth century, bounties were offered on the heads of 'miscreant' species (see chapter 4). Because of the destruction of their natural prey by settler hunting, some predators – mostly jackal and coyote – were forced into reliance on domestic stock. Other animals such as deer in North America, baboons and hippopotamuses (the latter also prized for its teeth which were used to make human dentures) trampled crops. Grazers like springbok and pronghorn antelope were thought to compete with stock for pasturage.[2]

Yet wildlife losses were reversible if habitat survived. Travellers and hunters noted the beaver's comeback in the American West two decades after the fashion change of the 1840s. Moreover, because of certain animals' adaptability, human intrusions sometimes led to temporary demographic surges. Wolves benefited for a while from the rich carrion of deer carcasses left by hide hunters. Once the wolf's forested and marshy habitat was cut back or drained, the smaller and highly opportunistic coyote profited at their expense – fanning out to occupy most of the wolf's historic range in North America. The coyote's South African counterpart was the jackal, which thrived on the spreading sheep flocks while its competitors such as the wild dog virtually disappeared. When eagles (including one commonly known as the *lammervanger*)[3] were harassed on account of their alleged taste for tender lamb, their main natural prey, the dassie (rock hyrax), multiplied and scuttled down from the hills to the plains. The regrowth of secondary (and tertiary) deciduous woodland with a profusion of browse in New England, as farmers went west, led to an upsurge in the white tail deer population. Hunters and death rates by no means determine the demographic fortunes of species. Birth rates, conditioned by habitat and adaptability, must be part of the equation.

If hunting was a necessary part of agrarian activities, it also inserted itself into less obvious areas of colonial expansion. Few historians have appreciated how wildlife resources could determine the pace and character of the frontier process. Wild meat subsidized a variety of intrusions, from missionary, military and whaling expeditions to mining and railroad construction. Expeditions for other purposes in southern Africa could offer plentiful fresh flesh shot en route as an inducement to reluctant porters and servants. By no means least, the availability of game facilitated the Voortrekkers' move out of the British Cape in the 1830s, relaxing their reliance on supply lines and large capital inputs. Frontier communities in both regions relished dried meat. In South Africa, indigenous methods were elaborated to produce salted, air-dried biltong – sometimes washed in vinegar – from a wide range of species. Its American cousin was jerky, while the durable pemmican (dried meat pounded by women and mixed with buffalo fat and sometimes berries) was the iron ration of Indian and white alike on the Plains. Prairie chicken and antelope were on the late nineteenth-century cowboy's menu more often than bacon and beans. Subsidy stretched to opportunistic scavenging by North American frontier farmers who drove their hogs to the killing fields to fatten on the leftovers of passenger pigeon and buffalo slaughters.

Throughout the nineteenth century, a compelling impulse behind the hunt for the visiting British élite was the idea of sport. In addition, as industrialization and urbanization reshaped economic and social life in the United States and, later, South Africa, a local élite expanded the reach of sports hunting. The status of wild animals was yet again recast, this time in less monetary terms. Progress in weapons technology from muzzle- to breech-loading and repeating rifle considerably enhanced killing capacity for all kinds of hunters during the 1870s. Swift oceanic steam transportation aided the adventurer as well as the emigrant, and the Panama-hatted Victorian Briton treated the American West as an informal extension of the empire, alluring not only to would-be beef barons with their gentlemanly capital but also to noble-born sportsmen who prized the buffalo, antelope and elk that the cattle kingdom was replacing. Recent literature on hunting has emphasized the predatory and seemingly pointless slaughter of colonial sports hunting. Harriet Ritvo (1987: 288) characterizes big game hunting as 'the most atavistic and antagonistic connection between humans and animals'. Much modern environmentalism is anti-hunting and the sports hunter provides a sitting duck for abuse. But this is an age of growing sensitivity to the rights of wild animals and it must be remembered that in those days hunting was the very essence and substance of sport.

Sporting adventures in Africa and the United States glided effortlessly into print and commanded a large sale in Europe. British hunters crossed the Atlantic drunk on J. Fenimore Cooper novels. R.G. Cumming was particularly adept at turning his exploits to literary and financial advantage. Happily combining pleasure and profit, he toured Britain in the 1850s displaying trophies and spoils. Subsequent hunters in southern Africa frequently invoked Cumming and Captain Cornwallis Harris. African hunting books sold just as well in the United States.

Cumming apparently found North American hunting too tame. Like many British bluebloods who had toured the empire, he lamented the absence of lions and tigers and considered buffalo an unchallenging adversary. His work even caught the eye of Henry David Thoreau, the famous American naturalist and proto-ecologist, who disapproved of hunting but included this genre in his reading. Like most Victorians, he was attracted by the celebration of savagery and believed he would enter into a more visceral relationship with the primitive through the act of killing: 'The African hunter Cumming tells us that the skin of the eland . . . emits the most delicious perfume of trees and grass' (1862: 610).

While the joys of the colonial chase usually involved small groups of mounted hunters with their retinues, the English custom of hunting with hounds was also adopted in both South Africa and America. Lord Charles Somerset ran a pack of hunting hounds at the Cape in the 1820s but they spread particularly rapidly when Frederick Carrington, colonel of the Bechuanaland police, started a pack at Mafikeng. In the absence of foxes, the jackal became their main quarry and it was considered an equal object of desire. In an expression of anglophilia, Wall Street brokers set up clubs on Long Island offering late-afternoon fox hunting; their hectic schedules demanded scented drags so it could all be over by dinnertime.

The red-blooded, arousing literary accounts that were distilled from these indulgences suggest that the British were unrivalled in their blithe and careless killing – and their books supply the most spectacular evidence of that destruction. The most celebrated of these elaborate hunting safaris in the US (whose outfitting provided a welcome fillip to frontier outpost economies) was Sir St George Gore's three-year, 6,000-mile procession through Colorado, Wyoming, Montana and the Dakotas (1854–6). A military official records the royal hunt arranged for the visiting Duke of Edinburgh in the Orange Free State when 600 antelope alone were slaughtered in a day. Gore, by contrast, only managed 2,000 buffalo and 1,600 deer and elk in almost three years (Spence, 1959: 56). Special excursion trains were laid on in both regions by the later nineteenth century so that armchair hunters could take pot shots. But this international sporting set was relatively small and while Africans and Native Americans had a different concept of sport, they undoubtably also enjoyed their hunting – and the status they derived from it. So did the pioneers.

Gentleman hunters, both visiting and resident, justified their activities not only by the pleasure derived but also by the contribution they were making to natural history. British hunters such as F.C. Selous, prominent in the last generation of commercial ivory-cum-sports hunters in southern Africa, devoted an increasing amount of their time to collecting for museums. Turn-of-the-century American travellers in search of adventure were predisposed to find a reincarnation of their own West in southern and eastern Africa (McCarthy, 1976–7). And African game was increasingly in the sights of American sportsmen after the American West lost much of its wildness toward the end of the nineteenth century. Gore's enterprise was rivalled in extravagance by Theodore Roosevelt. His profligate jaunt through British East Africa in 1909–10 – for which he was granted exemption from all game laws by the governor of Kenya – was sponsored by the Smithsonian. The ex-president's safari had been organized by Selous, who had hunted lynx and wolf in the US in the late 1890s. T.R. contributed a foreword to Selous's last book. Both were members of New York City's Ends of the Earth Club, which rolled hunting, taxidermy, science and adventure into one.

HUNTING CONTROLS

As élite hunters tried increasingly to establish a monopoly over game resources, tensions with subsistence and commercial hunters, both white and black, mounted. In South Africa, poorer Boers, pressurized by industrialization in the later nineteenth century, used remnant hunting opportunities to retain their autonomy from the labour market. 'The time has passed', Paul Kruger is supposed to have remarked in the 1880s, 'when a man could spend three days on the trail of a steenbuck instead of earning three pounds in this time' (Trapido, 1984). It was recognized that the capital to be generated from non-replaceable natural assets had a dwindling future. George Bird Grinnell, the patrician editor of the premier American sportsman's journal, *Forest and Stream*, editorialized in the same vein in 1894 – the year that action was taken to clamp down on poaching by market hunters in Yellowstone National Park. After acknowledging the role of hunting in frontier society ('For generations . . . it was right and proper, and wise and profitable that game should be killed for food') he proceeded: 'But times have changed . . . the day of game as an economic factor in the food supply of the country has gone by . . . we can now supply food with the plow and reaper and the cattle ranges cheaper than it can be furnished with the rifle' (Reiger, 1986: 70–1). Settler hunting was frowned upon by industrialists and more affluent farmers as a drag on economic progress. Trespass law was increasingly applied to defend private lands against intrusive hunting.

Hunting controls, in short, were designed to kill off competition. The opportunity to hunt operated as a safety valve and tonic that colonial officials were keen to preserve. Hunting helped make far-flung postings more desirable. Protecting game thus became part of the larger care of the empire. Considerations of social and racial control also operated in the US, where the élite strove similarly to exclude the lower classes, non-Anglo-Saxons and commercial hunting in general. This was the heyday of belief in their own biological and cultural supremacy based on the transfer to the social sphere of Darwinian notions of natural selection and survival of the fittest. Hunting controls were a way of asserting the white Anglo-Saxon protestant's imperial domain over increasingly multicultural and multiracial countries. Africans were criticized for the use of traps, nooses and deadfalls, like the poacher in rural England. American state regulations banning the use of lime and nets, imposing non-resident licence fees, barring aliens from carrying firearms in public (or owning them), and even from hunting altogether, expressed a revulsion against Italians, in whose cuisine cherished American songbirds were prominent.

From arrogating rights to game it was not a large step for the powerful to assume responsibility in a larger sense. Colonial regimes from Massachusetts to the Cape had been alive to the dangers of over-exploitation from the the earliest stages of settlement and quickly generated regulations along traditional European lines to conserve a usable stock. These embraced the closed season, protection of juveniles and outright bans on the taking of certain species (Leopold, 1933: 12–18). Nevertheless, European commentators remarked on the impoverishment of Cape game in the 1790s, including hyenas, elephants, rhino and various grazers. Even in the Boer Transvaal, where hunting was so critical to survival, the *Volksraad* (settlers' assembly) attempted to regulate for the wise usage and white monopoly of game from the 1850s. One rule specified that hunting should be for subsistence and kills restricted to one wagonload for every trip. African chiefs such as Khama of the Tswana and Lobengula of the Ndebele also tried to restrict hunting within their countries. Political authority was so dispersed and hunters so elusive that these measures were largely ineffectual.

By the late nineteenth century, the sports hunting fraternity recognized the failure of existing regulatory efforts and faced the alarming decline of game with a fresh urgency. The first crop of hunting clubs and protective associations in both regions date from the 1870s. The traditions of the British estate and the British hunting creed with its concept of the fair chase were re-created through private hunting reserves. If the medieval hunting park and chase of royalty and nobility provided a cultural reference point, nevertheless the modern version was more likely to be an associative or company venture that made opportunities available to the wealthy. In 1887, Theodore Roosevelt and other prominent New Yorkers founded the exclusive Boone and Crockett Club, dedicated to preservation in reserves of big game species such as bison, elk, mountain sheep and antelope. Soon afterwards, the Transvaal Game Preservation Association also combined the roles of hunting and agitating for the first reserves. Their imperial equivalent, The Society for the Preservation of the Wild Fauna of the Empire (SPWFE, 1907) – of which Roosevelt was an honorary member – consisted of the cream of the colonial establishment.

Other conservation orientated groups were emerging simultaneously in the United Kingdom. The Royal Society for the Protection of Birds (1891), a largely female initiative dominated by upper- and middle-class women, grew out of the fight against the plumage trade which was instigated in the 1880s by the American Audubon movement. Demonstrating the power of the purse, these Anglo-American women implemented what may qualify as the world's first 'green' consumer boycott (Merchant, 1985: 159–61). Once again, fashion came to the rescue. The survival of certain birds was assured in the 1920s when large ungainly hats – occasionally festooned with up to six entire stuffed birds – became extinct; the modish bob provided no anchorage for hatpins.

Members of the SPWFE were often characterized by sceptical contemporaries as 'penitent butchers'. Few, however, gave up hunting completely, repented, or apologized for the pleasure they continued to derive. Even when their role in game preservation is recognized, their interest has been dismissed as no more than a desire to perpetuate the supply of game for the sake of their sport's future. John MacKenzie (1988) draws a distinction for Africa between the narrow goal of game preservation and the broader concerns of wildlife conservation. In the American context, sportsmen campaigned not only for national forests, in which they could hunt, but also for wildlife refuges – where hunting was generally prohibited[4] – and national parks, which were to be covered by a blanket ban. As sportsmen argued then, and their historians claim now, sports hunting did not lead to any species' extinction.

Game reserves were established in both British colonies and Boer states from the 1880s. The Umfolozi, one of those established in Zululand in the 1890s, was specifically mandated to protect the remaining white rhino. In 1898, areas of the eastern Transvaal with a wide range of animal species were set aside as the Sabi reserve, an area later greatly extended. In 1900, representatives of the European powers with colonies in sub-Saharan Africa signed the Convention for the Preservation of Wild Animals, Birds and Fish in Africa. A German and

British initiative, it proclaimed total protection for a few species believed to be under threat of extinction, outlined restrictions on the taking of other species, prohibited certain methods of hunting and advocated game reserves.

Game reserves were initially delicate entities, limited in scope and aspiration. Designation (often by executive order) was a far cry from meaningful protection. Size was often nominal in the United States, where the first official reserve, Pelican Island, Florida (1903, to protect brown pelican nesting grounds), covered five acres. Reserves often faced acute local hostility. Deproclamations and reductions in size were common in the early twentieth century. Attitudes conducive to the disinterested protection of wildlife were as yet in their infancy and conceptions of the scale of land and management involved were rudimentary. Various historians have connected the emergence of greater sensitivity toward animals with the romantic movement of the late eighteenth and early nineteenth centuries (Thomas, 1983; Tuan, 1984; Turner, 1980). These changes, however, applied mostly to domestic creatures. Nor did the 'new' humanitarian movement that emanated from late nineteenth-century Britain to gain considerable influence in the US improve the status of wildlife, especially that of predators. The humanitarians wanted to eliminate beast's inhumanity to beast. Many were vegetarian and found flesh-eating animals abhorrent.

Another limitation of the game reserve from the modern environmentalist standpoint was the absence of an ecological grounding that recognized the value of the whole range of species. Far from being left to their natural devices, certain animals were privileged. The old and very broad farmers' definition of vermin to some extent traversed the boundaries of the game reserves. James Stevenson-Hamilton, the first warden of the Sabi reserve, was so anxious to restock the area that he advocated slaughter of predators such as leopards, lions, wild dogs and some reptiles, as well as controls over human hunters and poachers. Nor did 'outlaws' receive an amnesty in American refuges, many of which were designated for migratory wildfowl and managed to maximize their well-being; wardens not only restored wetlands but also shot owls and hawks. Similarly, American national parks were 'cleansed' of mountain lion (cougar) and wolf. Species identified as useful or desirable, by contrast, were deliberately bred and propagated for dispersal beyond the refuge.

Moreover, it was less a question of restoring wildlife populations to their original glory on a nationwide basis – however that may be measured – than a concern with salvaging certain relic animals in strictly defined areas. No longer a threat to civilization, these survivors could be spared as an expression of the generous ethics of a higher civilization. Elsewhere, it was business as usual, with little restraint on economic growth, national progress, or the idea of human supremacy. Reserves and parks simply became another, firmly subordinate category of land use, alongside the dominant private property. If an animal transgressed an invisible administrative line it reverted from protected wildlife to game or vermin up for grabs. The American national symbol, the 'lamb-eating' bald eagle, scourge of small furbearers and salmon, was only welcomed in from the cold in 1940 as a 'symbol of the American ideal of freedom' while the bounty on its white head in its last stronghold, Alaska, remained until 1945 (Robinson, 1975: 240).

Settler hunting practices, as well as hunting regulation, removed valuable food resources from indigenous peoples. During its nineteenth-century fever pitch, hunting also came close to destroying the wealth of species in both South Africa and the United States. Progress, as conceived by Europeans and their descendants, required a clean slate where new and largely imported patterns of production could be set down. The intricate and overbearing map of colonization threw into relief the unaccustomed new overlay of roads, towns and fences that demarcated private property. Not only native peoples got swept aside; even more so were the denizens of the pre-colonial 'old' world whose lairs, watering holes and killing fields had helped to define and structure the spatial relationships of the old landscape. Though some species and habitats survived in the interstices of the new material world, these were mostly in straitjackets and opportunities to regenerate were deeply constrained. Where springbok once roamed, only the Merino, dassie and jackal were to be found. The bison had given way to the Hereford. Once prominent features had been reduced to mere details.

NOTES

1 Polygamy, a characteristic feature of Plains Indian societies, was closely bound up with the robe trade. The more wives a man possessed to process the hides, the more buffalo he could kill.
2 Studies of pronghorn antelope food habits suggest they eat little grass, concentrating on weeds and shrubs, thus actually improving forage for cattle. A number of African antelope are browsers rather than grazers but this did not spare them either.
3 The term could refer to any eagle perceived to prey on domestic stock but is most closely associated with the black eagle.
4 US national (that is, federal) wildlife refuges were designed as sanctuaries, but parts of some have been opened to shooting at certain times of the year. Many states gave their approval for the purchase of lands for national refuges only on this condition. Outside federal lands, wildlife management

has been a state-level sphere of jurisdiction since independence. State refuges, financed largely by the sale of hunting and fishing licences, allow shooting. Sports hunters, through the purchase of 'duck stamps' and taxes on arms and ammunition, have contributed substantially to acquisition and management costs of state and national refuges since the 1930s.

REFERENCES AND FURTHER READING

Audubon, James (1831–9) (1971) in David D. Anderson (ed.), *Sunshine and Smoke: American Writers and their Environment*, Philadelphia: J.B. Lippincott.

Beinart, William (1990) 'Review article: Empire, hunting and ecological change in southern and central Africa', *Past & Present*, 128 (August), 162–86.

Brody, Hugh (1986) *Maps and Dreams*, London: Faber & Faber.

Caitlin, George (1844; 1989) *North American Indians*, 1989 edn edited by Peter Mathiessen, London: Penguin.

Carruthers, Jane (1988) 'Game protection in the Transvaal', unpublished Ph.D. thesis, University of Cape Town.

—— (1989) 'Creating a national park, 1910 to 1926', *Journal of Southern African Studies*, 15 (2), 188–215.

—— (1994) 'Dissecting the myth: Paul Kruger and the Kruger National Park', *Journal of Southern African Studies*, 220 (2), 263–84.

Cumming, R.G. (1856) *The Lion Hunter of South Africa: Five Years' Adventures in the Far Interior of South Africa*, London: John Murray.

De Kiewiet, C.W. (1941) *A History of South Africa, Social and Economic*, Oxford: Oxford University Press.

Elphick, R. (1985) *Khoi Khoi and the Founding of White South Africa*, Johannesburg: Ravan Press.

Fitter, Richard and Scott, Peter (1978) *The Penitent Butchers: Seventy-Five Years of Wildlife Conservation*, London: Collins.

Flores, Dan (1991) 'Bison ecology and bison diplomacy', *Journal of American History*, 78 (September), 465–85.

Gard, Wayne (1959) *The Great Buffalo Hunt*, Norman: University of Oklahoma Press.

Guy, J. (1980) 'Ecological factors in the rise of the Zulu kingdom', in S. Marks and A. Atmore (eds), *Economy and Society in Pre-Industrial South Africa*, London: Longman.

Hall, M. (1987) *The Changing Past: Farmers, Kings and Traders in Southern Africa, 200–1860*, Cape Town: David Philip.

Harris, W.C. (1839) *The Wild Sports of Southern Africa*, London: Bohn.

Irving, Washington (1835; 1985) *A Tour on the Prairies*, Norman: University of Oklahoma Press.

Lee, Richard (1979) *The !Kung San: Men, Women and Work in a Foraging Society*, Cambridge: Cambridge University Press.

Leopold, Aldo (1933) *Game Management*, New York: Charles Scribner's.

McCarthy, Michael (1976–7) 'Africa and the American West', *Journal of American Studies*, 11, 187–201.

MacKenzie, John (1988) *The Empire of Nature: Hunting, Conservation and British Imperialism*, Manchester: Manchester University Press.

Marks, Stuart A. (1993) *Southern Hunting in Black and White: Nature, History and Ritual in a Carolina Community*, Princeton: Princeton University Press.

Merchant, Carolyn (1985) 'The women of the progressive conservation crusade: 1900–1915', in Kendall E. Bailes (ed.), *Environmental History: Critical Issues in Comparative Perspective*, Lanham: University Press of America/American Society for Environmental History.

Merritt, John I. (1985) *Baronets and Buffalo: The British Sportsman in the American West, 1833–1881*, Missoula: Mountain Press.

Reiger, John (1986) *American Sportsmen and the Origins of Conservation*, Norman: University of Oklahoma Press.

Ritvo, Harriet (1987) *The Animal Estate: The English and Other Creatures in the Victorian Age*, Cambridge, Mass.: Harvard University Press.

Robinson, Glen O. (1975) *The Forest Service: A Study in Public Land Management*, Baltimore: Johns Hopkins University Press.

Roe, Frank Gilbert (1970) *The North American Buffalo*, Toronto: University of Toronto Press.

Sansom, B. (1974) 'Traditional economic systems', in W. Hammond-Tooke (ed.), *The Bantu-Speaking Peoples of South Africa*, Cape Town: Oxford University Press.

Sherwood, Morgan B. (1981) *Big Game in Alaska: A History of Wildlife and People*, New Haven: Yale University Press.

Skead, C.J. (1980) *Historical Mammal Incidence in the Cape Province*, vol. 1, Cape Town: Provincial Administration of the Cape of Good Hope.

Spence, Clark C. (1959) 'A Celtic Nimrod in the American West', *Montana: The Magazine of Western History*, 9 (Spring), 56–66.

Stevenson-Hamilton, James (1952, 1993) *South African Eden: The Kruger National Park 1902–1946*, Cape Town: Struik.

Taylor, S. (1989) *The Mighty Nimrod: A Life of Frederick Courteney Selous, African Hunter and Adventurer, 1851–1917*, London: Collins.

Thomas, Elizabeth Marshall (1958) *The Harmless People*, New York: Vintage.

Thomas, Keith (1983) *Man and the Natural World: Changing Attitudes in England, 1500–1800*, London: Penguin.

Thoreau, Henry D. (1862; 1985) 'Walking' in Carl Bode (ed.), *The Portable Thoreau*, London: Penguin.

Trapido, Stanley (1984) 'Poachers, proletarians and gentry in the early twentieth-century Transvaal', unpublished paper given at the African Studies Institute, University of the Witwatersrand.

Tuan, Yi-Fu (1984) *Dominance and Affection: The Making of Pets*, New Haven: Yale University Press.

Turner, James (1980) *Reckoning with the Beast: Animals, Pain and Humanity in the Victorian Mind*, Baltimore: Johns Hopkins University Press.

Wagner, R. (1980) 'Zoutpansberg: Some notes on the dynamics of a hunting frontier, 1848–1867', in S. Marks and A. Atmore (eds), *Economy and Society in Pre-Industrial South Africa*, London: Longman.

Wilmsen, E. (1993) *Land Filled with Flies*, Chicago: University of Chicago Press.

Wilson, Monica and Thompson, Leonard (eds) (1969) *The Oxford History of South Africa*, vol. 1, *South Africa to 1970*, Oxford: Clarendon Press.

Wishart, David (1979) *The Fur Trade of the American West: A Geographical Synthesis*, Lincoln: University of Nebraska Press.

3 The fall and rise of trees: forests, felling and forestry

Thick and intricate forest composed of a diverse range of hard and softwood species often dominates mental pictures of the North American physical environment. This leafy image is reinforced by recent films such as *The Last of the Mohicans*, based on the J. Fenimore Cooper novel (1826) set on the wilderness frontier of upstate New York, with its canopy of birch, beech, maple, hemlock, fir and spruce. By contrast, trees (and forests especially) rarely spring to mind when one pictures the South African natural world. Southern Africa does in fact support a large variety of trees and bushes, especially hardwoods, numbering nearly 900 species. But dense forest of big trees is the least extensive type of vegetational cover. The most heavily wooded areas were also those enjoying the highest rainfall – the sub-tropical forest along the east coast and the southern coast of the Cape.

Conventional statistics reinforce the notion of a sharp divergence between the proportion of forested land in our respective regions. Only a quarter of 1 per cent of South Africa remains under indigenous forest while little more than an additional 1 per cent is afforested in commercial plantations. Over 40 per cent of the land area of the contiguous United States, on the other hand, is estimated to have been wooded in 1492. The proportion of land under tree cover in the United States today amounts to a third – a figure well up on that of the early twentieth century. Yet we should look behind images and stark statistics. In the United States, trees have been – and remain – the dominant form of vegetation east of the Mississippi. The Pacific Northwest, which includes the world's biggest temperate rainforest in the Alaska panhandle, the Californian coastal ranges and slopes of the Sierra Nevada, are also heavily timbered. But notwithstanding these and lesser exceptions, many parts of the trans-Mississippi West are either treeless desert, semi-desert or grassland. In South Africa, the extensive Karoo region, as well as much of the highveld, has no forests, but the absence of forest does not always imply a dearth of trees and large shrubs. Through much of the region, except the highest and coldest spots, a wide variety of species occur dispersed in woodland and bushveld. Distinctions between a bush and a tree, woodland and forest – which deeply affect statistical notions – have shallow roots. Despite the certitudes of botanical definitions, these remain very much in the eye of the beholder.

While the nature of tree cover in our regions was very different, there are strong similarities in the impact of settlement and the uses to which wood was put by both pre-colonial and colonial societies. As in the case of wild animals, it is helpful to disaggregate the different processes impacting on woody vegetation. While some trees were chopped for their value as timber, from mastheads to musical instruments, others were cleared simply to make way for settlers' crops and cows. Similarly, the rationale for conservation from the later nineteenth century included a multiplicity of sometimes contradictory impulses, ranging from strategic factors and scientific fears to commercial considerations and aesthetic imperatives. This chapter will explore changing human reliance on trees and the arguments for their protection.

TREES AND PEOPLE

The degree of human dependency on trees for a surprising variety of basic needs is easily underestimated. Indigenous peoples and early settlers used trees for building, boats, fruit, shade, firewood, smoking food, medicine, dyes, armaments and art, to name but a few. Industrial techniques extended human capacity to harvest and commodify trees. While a plethora of new materials from concrete to plastics meant that people no longer had to lean so heavily on trees for basic needs, these time-honoured functions were seldom completely replaced.

Long-standing human interventions render the concept of 'natural' forest or woodland a thorny one. Traditional notions of ecosystem stability and climax, even before humans entered the picture, are being challenged. Climate change, geological convulsion, lightning and animal species could all radically alter the dynamic of vegetational change. Elephants, for example, uprooted trees and stripped bark, assisting the encroachment of bush at the expense of trees. They also 'planted' by spreading seed – their rich, warm dung furnished an ideal seedbed.[1] American scientists have argued, by contrast, that buffalo prevented tree growth on the prairie by trampling seedlings.

Clearing woodland for pasture and cultivation has been the most fundamental and widespread agent of human-induced environmental transformation in world history. This process was well advanced in the well-wooded coastlands of South Africa on the eve of European colonization. Travellers among the cattle-keeping, cultivating African chiefdoms commented on the patchwork of green pasture, fields and woodland in the rolling countryside between the Drakensberg and the sea. American Indians north of the Rio Grande had a lesser overall impact on the tree cover. Though they kept no domesticated pasturing animals, it is becoming clear that crops were a significant component of most tribal economies south of Maine – sometimes constituting up to half of their subsistence. Generally speaking, the larger the horticultural component in an indigenous economy, the greater the population density and, hence, the extent of tree clearance.

Hunter-gatherers burned to attract game but also gathered food from trees. The desert San of the Kalahari relied on the fruit of the mongongo tree. Anthropologist Lee noted that the !Kung, among whom he worked in the 1960s, gathered over half their subsistence from this tree. While men regaled each other with narratives from their hunting expeditions, women were occupied in the equally essential nut harvests. Acorn bread and mush was a staple of the fishing and hunting culture complex of coastal Californians. This type of gathering, however, did not involve damage to the source.

Agriculture, by contrast, required removal of trees. The most common methods employed (invariably men's work) were girdling, which cut off the flow of sap, and felling by fire. The roots were left to rot and in North America were later removed. Ash frequently served as a valuable fertilizer. Crops could be sowed immediately amid the charred stumps. At its most extreme, this system could involve forms of cultivation where seeds were sown in the ashbeds rather than the soil (*citimene* in central Africa). Fields were left fallow after a number of years. Secondary tree growth eventually blanketed the fallow area, especially in North America, though the composition was markedly different – fewer hardwoods and conifers. Shrinking fuelwood supplies as well as decline in soil fertility dictated the need to uproot settlements periodically – a decision usually taken by women in their capacity as primary gatherers and consumers.

Agriculture, however, was not the sole agent of deforestation under native regimes. Palisades and stockades demanded large quantities of wood. Various Algonkian tribes acquired the habit of living in log-houses from seventeenth-century Scandinavian settlers in the Delaware Valley, and all African buildings except on the most treeless parts of the highveld were largely of timber and reeds. The switch to wattle and daub or mud brick in the late nineteenth- and twentieth-century African building styles was partly a response to changing timber availability.[2]

As in the case of game and hunting, there has been long debate over the sustainability of pre-colonial timber harvesting, particularly in combination with shifting cultivation. Robert Moffat, the Scottish missionary who evangelized among the Tswana from the 1820s, was in the forefront of a South African tradition of criticizing profligate tree use by indigenous peoples. Tswana towns could reach population levels of over 10,000 people. According to Moffat, they were

> a nation of levellers – not reducing hills to comparative plains for the sake of building their towns, but cutting down every species of timber without regard to scenery or economy. . . . Thus when they fix on a site for a town, their first consideration is to be as near a thicket as possible. The whole is presently levelled, leaving only a few trees, one in each great man's field, to afford shelter from the heat and under which the mean walk and recline.
>
> (Grove, 1989: 169)

Changes stemming from contact with whites, and with the advance guard of introduced species that often preceded them, could intensify impacts. Buffalo-hunting tribes on the largely treeless American prairies extensively debarked cottonwoods and willows and cut down their saplings in riverine woodlands to provide winter fodder for their horses. There could be congregations in the early nineteenth century of up to 1,000 Indians with 20,000 horses and mules in winter camps like Big Timbers, Colorado (Sherow, 1992). Demands on timber multiplied as these congregations swelled in response to confinement on reservations. Southern Tswana chiefdoms, capitalizing on their investment into wagon transport, felled large numbers of camel thorns to supply the Kimberley mining market (Shillington, 1985: 102–6).

Moffat attributed the Tswana's devastating behaviour toward trees precisely to their heathenism. Commentators from the 1960s onwards, however, have stressed the eco-credentials of pagan religions. There certainly is evidence of a complex relationship between pre-colonial ideologies and tree preservation. Trees were believed to shelter spirits, especially in the religious systems of the Zimbabwean cults, who often located their shrines in groves. In the twentieth century, when colonial officials advocated 'clean' cultivation, that is completely cleared fields, to enhance yields, they faced local opposition (Wilson, 1989). Peasants objected, partly because they saw the value of trees in fields in terms of more instrumental features such as shade, humus and fruit (see chapter 6). Yet there was a strong religious overtone in that they were afraid of angering the spirit world. Ecological sensitivity in both North America and South Africa was often expressed by reference to ancestors and the protection of the 'hallowed' ground of burial sites.

Stepping outside the thicket surrounding the question of native spirituality and environmental attitudes, it seems clear that the slash and burn system worked tolerably in both regions while land was plentiful and people relatively sparse. The context changed rapidly with increasing numbers of colonists. In South Africa from the late nineteenth century, the growing number of African farmers cultivated increasingly restricted areas of land as whites encroached. Those remaining splintered groups of Native Americans were herded on to even more inconsequential lands from the standpoint of cultivation.

Wood served as an energy source for native and settler alike. Religious dissident Roger Williams, who broke away from the Massachusetts Bay Colony to found Rhode Island, related how (1643) the local Narragansett Indians surmised – on the basis of their own experience in denuding areas around their villages and wholesale removal on account of deforestation – that the English colonists had moved to New England because they had exhausted their fuel supplies at home (Merchant, 1993: 75). They were not far off the mark; European wood shortages from the sixteenth century were a factor compounding the misery that fostered emigration. Furthermore, new world fuelwood shortages were a local problem within ten to fifteen years of settlement. The superabundance of trees in New England encouraged profligacy in dwelling and hearth size, the favoured open fire of the New Englander being four to five times less efficient than the cast-iron closed stoves of the more restrained Pennsylvania Germans.

To an extraordinary extent, American settlers used wood for construction. The cedar shingle replaced thatch and slate while lumber substituted for brick. Yellowwood and stinkwood from the southern Cape coastal forests supplied floors and furniture in settlements such as Grahamstown. New England's distinctive stone walls actually date from the early nineteenth century – marking a reversion to the old world – appearing only after it became too expensive to maintain less durable wooden fences. In South Africa there was seldom enough local wood for fencing. But thorn bushes were cut to enclose animal kraals and durable sneezewood poles served as anchor posts when barbed wire fences snaked across the countryside in the late nineteenth century.

The most important non-domestic function for trees in colonial North America lay in ship-building and naval stores. Through this outlet the British colonies in America were pulled quickly into the international economy. White oak provided timbers and planking while the white pine furnished the best ship masts in the world. Naval supplies were protected by royal decree as early as 1691, trees of a certain size being marked with the so-called broad arrow (akin to a crow's foot). One surveyor of the royal woodlands apparently instructed militias fighting the Indians in the French and Indian Wars (1744–8) to watch out not only for Indians but to see if the trees they were hiding behind were suitable for masts (Malone, 1964: 193). There were accusations of waste, as majestically erect pines and cedars were chopped into shingles and canoes.

Restrictions on access to trees became a major source of cleavage that split colonists from Crown, not least because Boston had become a flourishing commercial centre. British policy interfered with a massive sawmill industry and thriving trade in planks and staves to supply barrels to the sugar plantations of the West Indies and the Atlantic 'wine islands' such as the Madeiras – themselves largely denuded by the late seventeenth century. Cape trees became a source of fuel for steamships plying the route to Asia and Australia, and the British authorities were also sufficiently worried about naval supplies there to set aside the (shortlived) Plettenberg Bay reserve amidst the region's richest forest resources on the southern Cape coast (1811).

Fresh, industry-geared uses of wood included material for rolling stock, stations, fences, bridges, trestle viaducts and sleepers (crossties). By 1890, an estimated 73 million of the latter were required each year in the United States to lay new lines and replace old ones; prior to chemical treatment, this had to be done every five to eight years (Pisani, 1985: 344). Riverboats and factories switching to steam also enhanced reliance on wood. Relative abundance meant that charcoal persisted as the basis for iron-smelting long after the Bessemer process was discovered. By the second half of the nineteenth century, Chicago, in its capacity as the nation's railroad hub, had become the nation's lumber centre, distributing trees from the Great Lakes region. The stands of white pine, the preferred sawtimber tree, were hacked down to carve open the treeless Plains of the western frontier; the famous sod-house (and straw bale) frontier has a restricted basis in reality.

The contemporary mind tends to equate deforestation with the massive commercial logging of tropical hardwoods in Amazonia and Southeast Asia. The commercial logging frontier in southern Africa was confined to relatively few zones yet this did not mean that trees were reprieved elsewhere. The success with sugar planting in coastal Natal, one of the regions best endowed with dense vegetation, permanently altered its landscape. In the United States, the logging frontier was more definable and identifiable. The cutting edge moved sharply from colonial New England to the Great Lakes in the pre-Civil War decades, then sliced down to the South after the war and slashed across to the Pacific Northwest at the end of the nineteenth century. But deforestation caused by commercial agriculture was more diffuse as trees tumbled before the axe and plough. In addition, crops such as tobacco, an American staple also grown in the Transvaal and Zimbabwe, required large amounts of wood for curing leaves.

Technological change had an appetite for timber but could also relieve pressure on particular species or areas. The arrival of the railway in Kimberley in 1884, and with it imported coal carried a thousand kilometres over land, saved the semi-arid region's timber from further depletion. Mining triggered widespread timber plantations in the late nineteenth century. Even so, the Rand goldmines could not depend heavily on wood for fuel and their expansion generated a rapidly growing coal industry. The major power utility on the Rand was named the Victoria Falls Power Company, in the vain hope that hydroelectric provison would be possible but coal remained king, whose dirty, acrid reign continues. The mushrooming mines and company towns of America consumed large quantities of wood, pockmarking the face of the frontier. Their capacity to be supported by wood lasted longer than in South Africa but coal, electricity and steel eventually eradicated timber's value to the American mining industry.

The often unintentional exchange of plants that Crosby regards as a prominent feature of colonization was later complemented – and sometimes even outweighed – by systematic, commercially and scientifically informed botanic importation. In view of South Africa's perceived lack of quick maturing, straight trunked species, importation was given priority. The United States with its wealth of easily worked softwoods was largely self-sufficient in this department except in the more arid West. Conifers from the temperate northern hemisphere were one solution to natural 'deficiency' but it was the Australian wattle and eucalyptus ('gum') that dominated the new floral community in South Africa and to a lesser extent in places like California. Fast growing (up to twenty feet in four years), stump sprouting, drought resistant and shade providing, these readily naturalized antipodean migrants acculturated happily in relatively poor soil. In California, the gum provided many of the state's railroad crossties, and in South Africa they were also used for telegraph poles and pit props – the mining industry currently consumes 20 per cent of the country's tree production. In early twentieth-century Zimbabwe, mine owners were given virtual *carte blanche* to snap up timber not only from the land they owned but also from farmland owned by other whites.

The black wattle spread over most of Natal from the 1860s onwards and into the Transvaal, its expansion subject to sufficient rainfall and absence of frost. Initially introduced as a source of household timber and fuel, as well as a windbreak and shade tree for livestock, it began to be planted specifically for tanbark in the 1870s. Wattle provided the basis for tanning, one of the relatively few domestic industries in the nineteenth century. Varieties of this highly adaptable exotic were also marshalled to stabilize the drifting sands of the Cape Flats. Not least, the wattle became the staple of woodlots in the African districts of the Transkeian territories. Stands were cultivated for fuel and building materials, moulding the very shape of vernacular architecture (Sherry, 1971). Plantations often whittled away at grassland as well as muscling into existing woodland. Wattle and gums were thus a major factor in the demise of certain wildlife. Few indigenous animal species could survive on gum browse. The trees now stand accused of lowering water tables and sucking up springs, even of causing soil erosion.

Agave (the century plant) with its sharp-tipped, serrated leaves, was imported to South Africa from the southwestern US and Mexico, where it had been a painful obstacle to European exploration, sometimes impaling riders. (It remains a scourge, much to the delight of desert preservationists, puncturing tyres of off-road vehicles.) In South Africa, the spiked agave was planted as kraal fencing to restrain cattle. It excelled as an anti-erosion device both because it grew on inhospitable soil and prevented livestock grazing in gullies; chopped, it served as animal feed in times of drought.

John Croumbie Brown, Cape Botanist and leading South African conservationist in the 1860s, used Darwinian arguments in his campaign for the introduction of the fittest, all-conquering eucalyptus (Grove, 1989: 184). Enthusiasts such as Brown might not, however, have anticipated some of the the consequences of the exotic supertrees. Tamarisk was introduced from North Africa into the American southwest for shade and shelterbelts, and has since gone feral, gumming up indigenous vegetation. Another variety of tamarisk from Asia, introduced at the turn of the century because of its penchant for wet areas along streams, reservoirs and irrigation ditches, which apparently equipped it for erosion control, also escaped and has so far resisted eradication. Everywhere, the eucalyptus, much lauded in the nineteenth century, is regarded as an environmental *arbor non grata* because of its deep thirst and desiccating tendencies. In the western Cape, exotics such as the pine and hakea have invaded the extraordinarily hetero-geneous and sensitive fynbos zones.

An intriguing feature of modern environmentalism in both regions is botanical xenophobia, a desire to reassert the interests of the old stock in the face of a choking influx of fitter foreign breeds. This pre-occupation with original purity and biodiversity rejects the international dynamism of ecological succession, raising knotty questions: does nature aspire to pristine perfection? Can aliens ever be naturalized? It is difficult to sustain an argument that all botanical immigrants should be uprooted and repatriated. If this were done, the United States would have to subsist on tortillas and refried beans, South Africa on springbok burgers. The fruit trees originally grown from cuttings carefully carried westward by American pioneer women (Kolodny, 1984), alongside other treasured possessions, would have to be torn out. Frangipanis and loquats, eastern exotics which have long beautified Cape gardens and have come to characterize them, would disappear. So would the vineyards of California and the Cape. But just as these countries' biological diversity has probably been enriched by importation, the success of particular plants threatens the variety of indigenous life. So there must be a strong case for control of rampant invaders, even for eradication in niches specially set aside for attempts to nurture indigenous splendour.

FORESTRY AND CONSERVATION

For a number of centuries in the United States, a land where labour was scarce and natural resources abundant, the conservation of human energy was more important than the preservation of trees. Whereas the Native Americans of California shook or knocked down their acorns, this went against the settler grain. An incredulous European visitor to New Jersey in the 1790s reported that settler Americans 'in order to save themselves the work of shaking or pulling off the nuts . . . find it simpler to cut the tree and gather the nuts from it, as it lies on the ground' (as quoted in Jacobs, 1980: 51). If forests were destroyed for economic reasons they were conserved for economic reasons too. The first colonial forest reserves in both regions, like hunting rules, conformed to a long European tradition of conserving dwindling natural resources.

In 1626, a mere six years after its founding, Plymouth Colony began to regulate cutting, as did Dutch officials around Cape Town in the seventeenth century. Even at this stage, colonists planted trees; Governor Simon van der Stel initiated the planting of 16,000 oak trees at the Cape and, though exotics, they became a symbol of settlement and colonial civilization. Forestry seems to display a similar evolution to the control of game resources, from regulation over cutting to the creation of reserves. The aforementioned South African venture of 1811 at Plettenberg Bay was soon deproclaimed, as were the earliest US federal government initiatives around the same time. Following severe drought in South Africa between 1845–7 and growing publicization of the destruction of old growth forest like the cedar of the Cedarberg mountains, new forest conservancies sprouted in the 1850s, along with measures to prevent veld burning.

Grove would splice these Cape initiatives on to a longer history of imperial tree protection. He argues that the economic consequences of environmental degradation emerged most strikingly on the islands along the major trade and shipping routes in the seventeenth and eighteenth centuries. Colonial administrators were forced to grapple with the inability of waystations such as Mauritius and St Helena to function as suppliers of wood, food and water. Deforestation, above all, made a big impression and forced some of the world's most comprehensive early conservationist legislation (Grove, 1990).

By the mid-nineteenth century, scientific thinking about desiccation had entered forestry debates. Desiccation theory was nothing new and had its roots in folk belief. A strong argument for forest clearance on the northeastern American seaboard was the moderating (that is, drying and warming) influence on a climate considered too cold and wet by British agricultural standards. From the observations of eighteenth-century New England commentators it transpired that deforestation dried out the soil and rendered the land hotter in summer and colder in winter – the reverse of what was hoped for! They also noted how clearance increased wind force, and rates of evaporation and runoff. This resulted in greater incidence of flooding and irregular stream flow.

During the second half of the nineteenth century, science formally identified the relationship between tree cover, rainfall and soil erosion. British officials in India linked deforestation to the threat of drought and desiccation. By the late nineteenth century, the old view that deforestation had a direct effect on climate and rainfall was widely canvassed. When thousands of lives were lost in the Johnstown, Pennsylvania flood of 1889, watershed deforestation was immediately recognized as the cause.[3]

F.E. Kanthack, an imperial offical who moved from India to the Cape in 1907 to take charge of irrigation affairs, believed not only that forests were critical in preventing soil erosion and siltation but subscribed firmly to the view that forests increased rainfall. For if clearing was thought to warm and dry up the climate, the converse was also believed: that planting trees would render arid regions cooler and moister. According to this theory, tree roots tapped groundwater which was then released through foliage, cooling passing air which encouraged condensation. Furthermore, their canopies reduced heat escape which lowered temperatures. American foresters and scientists who shared this scientific orthodoxy encouraged settlers on the Plains to plant trees in the latter part of the nineteenth century. The Timber Culture Act (1873) enshrined this belief by granting homesteaders an extra 160 acres if they would plant 40 of these acres with trees. Arbor Day, the annual community tree-planting ceremony – now also established in South Africa – began in treeless Nebraska around the same time.

Scientific and economic concerns were to some extent fused in the mid-century Cape. Ludwig Pappe, an Austrian who served as official Cape Botanist between 1858 and 1862, was one of the first in that region to raise the alarm over the condition of forest and range. He was particularly worried about veld and forest fires (burning by graziers to encourage new growth) during the dry years of the 1850s. The seeds of conservation thinking produced early green shoots in the 1859 Cape Forest and Herbage Protection Act – one of the most advanced for its time. The Cape government continued to take the lead in the region, funding a 'Superintendent of Woods and Forests' in 1880 – a model subsequently imposed unmodified on the rest of the region. The authoritarian nature of colonial regimes facilitated unilateral state action. By contrast, the combination of weak central and strong local state governmental traditions, not to mention an ethos of unrestrained popular capitalism, tended to stump American initiatives. Unsurprisingly, early ventures were confined to private lands such as the railroad tycoon George Vanderbilt's estate in North Carolina.[4]

Scientific arguments also kindled American government action at this time. The major arguments were assembled by George Perkins Marsh in his seminal book *Man and Nature; or, Physical Geography as Modified by Human Action* (1864), much of which was a cautionary environmental history of Europe based on extensive travel and scholarship. Marsh focused on the desiccating role of grazing and deforestation arguing that these were integral factors in the collapse of ancient Greece and Rome. Pappe's successor as Cape Botanist, John Croumbie Brown (1862–6), used similar arguments (though not derived from Marsh) in his propaganda for more wholesale programmes involving soil, water, forest and species conservation. And Marsh, with whom he corresponded, encouraged Brown to publish his various observations and researches, which appeared as *The Hydrology of South Africa* (1875) (Grove, 1987: 32).

These various pioneering ventures predated the best-known phase of early forestry as implemented by the American government in the final decades of the nineteenth century, and from which Gifford Pinchot is inseparable. American conservation history has revolved around this topic to an inordinate degree; this truncated version even regards conservation as a phenomenon to be Pinchot's invention. Though Pinchot slighted the contribution of non-American precursors, extra-European forestry was grounded in well-established old world practices. The Cape authorities appointed a French expert (De Vasselot) as their first Superintendent of Woods and Forests, and a German was the first equivalent in the Transkeian Territories. Similarly, the first American forester was a Prussian, Bernard Fernow, who served as chief of the forestry division, US Department of Agriculture. Other conservation-minded federal officials in the 1870s and 1880s also tended to be fellow-immigrants who injected into American natural resource management the more mature European perspective of maintaining a balance between rates of growth and harvest.[5]

Moreover, in the absence of an American forestry school, Pinchot was obliged to attend the French imperial forestry school at Nancy (founded in 1824), where the budding young forester studied the rigorous French, German and Swiss traditions. But the most direct and immediate influence on Pinchot and American forestry was British India – the metropole being overwhelmingly dependent on colonial plantations for its timber needs. Indian-trained conservators joined Europeans in the emerging South African forestry bureaucracy. And Pinchot, whose mentor was Sir Dietrich Brandis, the Prussian-born chief of the Indian Imperial Forest Department, eventually conceded in his autobiography (*Breaking New Ground*, 1947) that the term 'conservation' was inspired by the British forest conservancies. (The term had hitherto been restricted chiefly to the preservation of fruit and the keeping of bees.) Yet the debate over where, with whom, and precisely when forestry originated is less important for our purposes than it is to note the transnational emergence of forestry as a profession. From European roots it branched out into a network of contacts, ideas, experiences, responses, expertise and journals. Nurseries for tree managers ranged from Yale Forestry School (set up in 1900 with Pinchot family money) to Oxford University's Department of Forestry which, funded by the colonial office, became the Imperial Forestry Institute in 1924.

Forestry in some cases involved the protection of indigenous species and of watersheds in general but its mission was increasingly the commercial propagation of trees. The rationale behind conservation in the late nineteenth-century United States was concern over the continuing health of the national economy – even the future of American civilization and great nation status itself. As Fernow warned in 1902: 'A nation may cease to exist as well by the decay of its resources as by the extinction of its patriotic spirit' (Merchant, 1993: 349). Imperial forest management, in similar fashion, was governed by the fact that Britain imported over 90 per cent of its timber requirements in the early twentieth century. Colonial foresters, trained in Britain, were keenly aware of both local and metropolitan timber requirements. Forestry became stoutly utilitarian, reflecting both imperial and Progressive American ideas of managing the colonial/national estate. Since the majority saw forests as tree farms, it made sense that the US forest service (1905) was located within the Department of Agriculture. In the Cape, a department for forestry (1876) predated provision for agriculture and only became absorbed by the latter for a period of some twenty years.

At the Cape, De Vasselot systematically introduced pine plantations arranged in blocks. Pinchot's admiration for the neatly organized French forests he studied while at Nancy was transplanted into a vision of American trees as crops in easily harvested, renewable rows. The forest service he headed envisaged a partnership with the corporate world, supplying information to railroad companies, for example, on the relative merits of various woods for trestles and crossties. Contrary to traditional historiography, and populist packaging aside, the desire to bust rapacious robber barons was not a strong ingredient in US forest conservation, which was often heartily supported by those who appreciated the virtues of regulation and production control at a time when there was a glut of timber and chronic competition. The most vigorous opponents who squealed about 'Prussian methods' were pioneer types feeling squeezed out by the increasing rationalization and cartelization of business.

Utilitarian and aesthetic conservation could be contained within the same vessel but there was a tendency – much stronger in the United States – for the debate to become split. Those who wanted to let nature run wild in the US national forests (the first batch were established in 1891) were a marginalized minority labelled as romantic aesthetes or preservationists – though they too envisaged a permanent role for central government in protecting nature. While the utilitarian ethos held sway, this preservationist tributary, only a trickle at the time, deserves attention because it would swell into the main channel of modern environmentalism (see chapter 6).

An equally distinctive undercurrent latched on to botanical diversity and a more aesthetic and holistic approach survived in the colonial and

South African forestry services. Protagonists proclaimed the moral evil of deforestation:

> it is the opinion of a large number of people that the destruction of the forests means the deterioration of the most fertile and the disfigurement of the only beautiful parts of the country. . . . It is as much the moral duty of a civilized government to set its face against forest destruction . . . . as it is to discountenance any other social evil, such as slavery or witchcraft.
>
> (Hutchins quoted in Grove, 1989: 185)

American female pioneers were possibly more sensitive than men to the glories of wild landscapes. Their published reflections on frontier life refer to their distaste for the male tendency to chop down every single tree around homesteads; they preferred beauty and shade (Kolodny, 1984). Some propounded the value of wild nature as a tonic for the jaded human spirit in the form of a recreational amenity. There was certainly no South African equivalent to John Muir, the standard-bearer of US aesthetic conservation, in terms of public reception, political influence (though he never held government office) and the uncompromising nature of his wilderness preservation argument. This often incendiary language occasionally surfaces in South African debates but more passionately with regard to wild animals.

The utilitarian hegemony over tree conservation, whose kernel was the elimination of waste and needless destruction, is perhaps exemplified by attitudes to fire. Debris left in cut-over areas was a tinder box while locomotive sparks, negligent hunters, and stockmen's burning all exacerbated the problem. Action to manage forests at the state level typically rose from the ashes of catastrophes such as the Hinkley, Minnesota, fire of 1894, which left 418 people dead. The centrality of fire prevention to notions of forest conservation in the US is illustrated by the success of Smokey the Bear. The icon was born in the mid-1940s and the crusade turned up the heat in 1950, when a bear cub found orphaned (presumably) by a forest fire was shipped off to the national zoo to serve the rest of his life as a symbol for fire protection. Smokey's South African equivalent, still on many signboards, was a doleful, Bambi-like baby antelope.[6]

Kanthack, Director of Irrigation at the Cape, bemoaned the fate of expensive dams and irrigation schemes, silting up at an alarming rate due to devegetation of their watersheds. In the early twentieth century, the Chief Conservator of Forests in the Orange Free State advocated extensive afforestation to secure the water supply in the great westward flowing rivers of the Caledon and Orange. Watershed protection – to ensure adequate water levels for navigation on the commercially vital Hudson River and Erie Canal – was the major force behind the setting up of the Adirondack state park in once thickly wooded upstate New York (1885).

By and large, early twentieth-century plantations on both state and private lands in South Africa catered for commercial timber consumers. The largest demand by rural Africans, however, was for local access to wood for fuel and other subsistence needs. The government forestry department was by no means deaf to these requirements. In the vicinity of larger plantations, Africans were allowed to collect windfalls. More important, prescient foresters in the African-settled Transkeian Territories planted devolved woodlots and encouraged tree planting around homesteads. African headmen were left in control of some small areas of indigenous woodland. By the time of the Imperial Forestry Conference held in Johannesburg in 1935, the idea of communal planted woodlots was gaining ground. In both regions, the role of trees within the agricultural land-use category was recognized, and extension services began to promote farm forestry in the early twentieth century. During the 'dirty thirties' on the US Great Plains, trees were touted as an alternative to cotton on played-out private lands. The greening of timber culture through notions of agroforestry in contemporary development ideology is by no means entirely new.

The main thrust of forestry in both the United States and South Africa unarguably remains planting and cutting of commercial timber. In so far as it involves the replacement of indigenous vegetation, this is often judged a destructive activity; less than a fifth of American forests today are classified as 'old growth'. Yet forestry has grown more multifaceted and imaginative. The role of relatively undisturbed woodland in providing habitat for a wide range of creatures, as well as plant biodiversity, has been steadily winning support since the Second World War (see chapter 6). The doctrine of multiple use, formally enacted through US legislation in 1960, also involved recognition of the recreational significance of forests in a wild state. Elements within the US Forest Service had actually taken the lead here during the interwar period with the designation of a half-million-acre wilderness reserve within Arizona's Gila National Forest (1924). Moreover, in southern Africa, proponents of small-scale agroforestry directed to the immediate needs of rural consumers have gained a voice. Foresters are increasingly looking beyond timber as a commodity and corporations as their clientele, to glimpse the complex interdependence of societies, nature and trees.

NOTES

1 The humble mopane worm (a type of caterpillar) may be even more important than the elephant in fertilizing parts of the Transvaal. A recent estimate suggests that an average population of worms could evacuate a quarter million rands worth of dung on 1,000 hectares in little more than a month (Styles, 1994).

2 The term 'wattle and daub' predates the use of wattle to describe a specific Australian species. Hence, wattle and daub structures could be built with any suitable tree.

3 Desiccation theory continues to be argued over as a factor in global, as distinct from local, climate change.

4 Forests on private lands, which includes farm woodlands as well as plantations, still constitute the great bulk of commercial timber in the USA.

5 This form of forest management is echoed in current notions of sustainable development.

6 One outcome of a more recent biocentric approach has been a partial reappraisal of attitudes to fire within national parks. Tourists making their once-in-a-lifetime visit to Yellowstone in the summer of 1988 were appalled to find fires obscuring the famous views. They derived little comfort from the assurance that this short-term destruction and aesthetic blight was ecologically constructive in the longer term.

REFERENCES AND FURTHER READING

Brown, John C. (1875) *Hydrology of South Africa*, Edinburgh: Henry King.

Carlson, K. (1913) 'Forestry in relation to irrigation in South Africa', *Agricultural Journal of the Union of South Africa*, V, 219–34.

Cox, Thomas R., Maxwell, Robert S., Thomas, Phillip Drennon and Malone, Joseph J. (1985) *This Well Wooded Land: Americans and Their Forests from Colonial Times to the Present*, Lincoln: University of Nebraska Press.

Cronon, William (1983) *Changes in the Land: Indians, Colonists, and the Ecology of New England*, New York: Hill & Wang.

Grove, Richard (1987) 'Early themes in African conservation: the Cape in the nineteenth century', in D. Anderson and R. Grove (eds) *Conservation in Africa: People, Policies and Practice*, Cambridge: Cambridge University Press.

—— (1988) 'Conservation and colonial expansion: a study of the evolution of environmental attitudes and conservation policies on St Helena, Mauritius and in India, 1660–1860', Ph.D. dissertation, University of Cambridge.

—— (1989) 'Scottish missionaries, evangelical discourses and the origins of conservation thinking in Southern Africa 1820–1900', *Journal of Southern African Studies*, 15 (2) (January), 163–87.

—— (1990) 'The origins of environmentalism', *Nature*, 345 (3 May), 11–14.

Hays, Samuel P. (1959) *Conservation and the Gospel of Efficiency: The Progressive Conservation Movement, 1890–1920*, Cambridge, Mass.: Harvard University Press.

Henkel, C. C. (1903) *The Native or Transkeian Territories*, Cape Town: Juta & Co.

Jacobs, Wilbur R. (1980), 'Indians as ecologists', in Christopher Vecsey and Robert W. Venables (eds), *American Indian Environments: Ecological Issues in Native American History*, Syracuse: Syracuse University Press.

Kanthack, F.E. (1908) 'The destruction of mountain vegetation: its effects upon the agricultural conditions in the valleys', *Agricultural Journal of the Cape of Good Hope*, XXXIII (2), 194–204.

—— (1909) 'Irrigation development in the Cape Colony, past, present and future', *Agricultural Journal of the Cape of Good Hope*, XXXIV (6), 645–57.

Kolodny, Annette (1984) *The Land before Her: Fantasy and Experience of the American Frontiers 1630–1860*, Chapel Hill: University of North Carolina Press.

Malone, Joseph J. (1964) *Pine Trees and Politics: The Naval Stores and Forest Policy in Colonial New England, 1691–1775*, London: Longman.

Marsh, George Perkins (1864) (1965 edition) *Man and Nature*, Cambridge, Mass.: Harvard University Press.

Merchant, Carolyn (ed.) (1993) *Major Problems in American Environmental History*, Lexington: D.C. Heath.

Pinchot, Gifford (1947) *Breaking New Ground*, New York: Harcourt, Brace.

Pinkett, Harold T. (1970) *Gifford Pinchot: Private and Public Forester*, Urbana: University of Illinois Press.

Pisani, Donald J. (1985) 'Forests and conservation, 1865–1890', *Journal of American History*, 72 (2) (September), 340–59.

Ranger, T.O. (1985) 'Religious studies and political economy: the Mwari cult and the peasant experience in Southern Rhodesia', in W. van Binsbergen and J.M. Schoffeleers, *Theoretical Explorations in African Religions*, London: Routledge & Kegan Paul.

—— (1989) 'Whose heritage?: the case of Matobo National Park', *Journal of Southern African Studies*, 15 (2), 217–49.

Sherow, James E. (1992) 'Workings of the geodialectic: High Plains Indians and their horses in the region of the Arkansas River Valley, 1800–1870', *Environmental History Review*, 16 (Summer), 61–85.

Sherry, J.S. (1971) *The Black Wattle*, Pietermaritzburg: University of Natal Press.

Shillington, K. (1985) *The Colonisation of the Southern Tswana 1870–1900*, Johannesburg: Ravan Press.

Sim, T.R. (1907) *The Forests and Forest Flora of the Cape Colony*, Aberdeen: Taylor & Henderson.

Steen, Harold K. (1976) *The U.S. Forest Service: A History*, Seattle: University of Washington Press.

Styles, Chris (1994) 'Mopane worms: more important than elephants?', *Farmer's Weekly* (South Africa), 29 July, 14–16.

Williams, Michael (1989) *Americans and Their Forests: A Historical Geography*, New York: Cambridge University Press.

Wilson, K. (1989) 'Trees in fields in Southern Zimbabwe', *Journal of Southern African Studies*, 15 (2), 369–83.

4 Agriculture: exploitation unlimited and limited

EXPLOITATION UNLIMITED

The hunting frontier and deforestation had their own dynamics shaped by sport, trade and lumbering. But both, we have contended, were intimately related to another process of ecological transformation – the expansion of agriculture, especially of the settler, commercial variety. The farming of new crops and animals has arguably most altered the physical environment of both regions as well as having produced some of the most complex regulation. The Dust Bowl of the early 1930s which accompanied the depression on the Great Plains dominates discussion of American agriculture in mainstream environmental history. Aeolian erosion, captured in images of swirling storms blackening out the noonday sun and of fence posts topped by sand drifts, found scholarly expression in apocalyptically titled books. The epitome was *Deserts on the March* (1935) by the Oklahoma botanist Paul Sears.

Those few who have dealt with the topic in South Africa – where there was a similar environmental disaster in the 1930s – rely heavily on the doom-laden and portentous language of the Drought Commission. This was a key document in analysis of the ecological problems caused by settler stock farming which pictured 'a great South African desert in the making' (Drought Investigation Commission, 1922: 2). The term was taken from the Great American Desert, marked on early-nineteenth-century maps as the region between the 98th meridian and the Rockies. Ironically, this referred to American land that had not yet been colonized – and which many thought never could be because God had made it so – as opposed to land that had been laid waste by settler occupation. (By the time of the Drought Commission's investigations, man rather than God or nature was blamed for barren land.) When two British colonial soil scientists, G.V. Jacks and R.O. Whyte, attempted a comparative international view of soil erosion in the 1930s, they called their book *The Rape of the Earth* (1939) and pinpointed the USA and South Africa as two of the most degraded zones. They regarded the South African situation as more urgent, however, for the American authorities appeared to be doing more about it.

Easy as it is to view the dust storms as the logical culmination of three centuries of land abuse – and longer if indigenous practices are taken into account – environmental destruction by agricultural enterprise precedes this dramatic moment and has a complex and varied history. Moreover, this teleological and fatalistic view of the 1930s with its heavy accent on degradation is conceptually unsatisfactory. Soil exposure and erosion can occur through natural agency such as fire, drought, geological forces and animal burrowing. Human activity intensifies these processes and while settler agriculture has been responsible for major environmental losses, by no means all of it has been irreversible. The most vigorous academic defence of settler agriculture in the United States was issued by pioneering ecological historian James Malin during the 1930s and after. He argued in the most partisan fashion that environmental change stemming from human occupation of grasslands was incremental rather than fundamental in its impact. Furthermore, in South Africa and the United States, there was some recognition from an early stage of the need to contain and control the most profligate features of settler agriculture.

Despite the apparent squander of natural bounty, both countries have maintained their status among the limited range of net exporters of agricultural commodities. It is true that in both countries relative plenty has been maintained through energy-intensive and potentially polluting techniques. In South Africa, at least, food security in the midst of surplus has by no means been assured for poorer black communities. None the less, we must guard against the glib polemics of environmental despair. If environmental historians stalk the past with only one idea – despoliation – in their minds, and just one word – degradation – in their vocabulary, then they would find it difficult to account for and describe the reconstruction and restabilization of the natural world in various guises. A notion of transformation should be set alongside that of destruction.

As we have sought to show, indigenous peoples actively fattened the land rather than simply lived off its fat. The location and availability of natural resources deeply constrained human agrarian capacity. On the well-watered and hilly countryside of the South African east coast, where hundreds of rivers tumbled down from the Drakensberg to the sea, African settlement could be dispersed and fields scattered in choice soil near the homesteads. The shortage of water supply in the flatter lands of the interior highveld led to more concentrated settlements and lands. Rainmaking rituals came into their own both to propitiate the ancestors who traversed and protected the land as well as to bind the community at crucial moments in the agriculture cycle. But even with their limited range of pre-colonial crops (sorghum, pumpkins and beans) and homemade iron hoes, this was a form of agriculture whose imprint was firm and long-lasting. Contrary to their own myths of moving into empty and unkempt lands, settlers found fields and prepared veld as well as wilderness.

Certain American Indian tribes, where climate and soils permitted, also practised fairly systematic (if shifting) cultivation; somewhat surprised early settler accounts detailed the size, diversity and productivity of husbandry in the Chesapeake. In both regions, early settlers and missionaries frowned on the subjugation of women in indigenous agriculture. The myth of the lazy African man squatting under the proverbial tree honing his assegai (spear) fed their sense of righteousness in dispossessing incumbents. In some instances where disease ravaged Indian communities in North America, early settlers, like cuckoos raising their young in the nests of other birds, planted in fields they had not prepared and harvested what they had not sown.

One of the most fascinating exchanges between the continents involved the adoption by Africans not only of maize as an increasingly central staple in the nineteenth century, but the wholesale transfer of the 'corn, beans and squash' food complex. This complementary farming system, probably initially transferred on early Portuguese ships, enormously facilitated the expansion of African agriculture. Until very recently, fields on the east coast settlements of South Africa could be found with nitrogen-fixing bean stalks entwined around the maize, while, at ground level, pumpkin leaves suffocated weed growth and cooled the soil.

The transforming effects of new farmers, crops and techniques which took root the instant the settlers disembarked, however, are the processes that have engaged recent historical attention. Crosby argued robustly that Europeans' plants and animals formed 'part of a grunting, lowing, neighing, crowing, chirping, snarling, buzzing, self-replicating and world-altering avalanche' (Crosby, 1986: 194). (American Indians regarded the buzzing of the honey bee as harbinger of the white man.) The ecological niches vacated by wildlife driven to the brink by settler hunting were reoccupied by domestic stock and transformed in the process. Proliferating cattle in North America, in their pursuit of *lebensraum*, invaded and destroyed Indian crops, while pigs competed directly for acorns and clams. Colonists would deliberately set stock to encroach on native-held territory and foodstuffs.

Clashes over domestic animals exacerbated and epitomized land-use conflicts between native peoples and settlers. Lacking livestock, Native Americans did not recognize private property in animals – domestic or wild – especially when allowed to roam free, as most pigs were: an animal was only owned when killed. San also took the domestic stock of both Africans and whites as free goods. The first great frontier wars between the colonists and the cattle-rich Xhosa in the eastern Cape were fought partly over the *zuurveld*, the area's prime seasonal grazing. European germs communicated to native peoples had their counterpart in diseases such as brucellosis, anthrax and tuberculosis transmitted from cattle to American wildlife. The traffic in diseases could be in the opposite direction in South Africa, where trypanosomiasis carried by wild animals inflicted itself on settler cattle. But the introduced epidemic of rinderpest in the 1890s wiped out large quantities of antelope as well as cattle.

In many areas settlers adopted indigenous techniques and knowledge. Maize and potatoes (though now cultivated by plough) are critical examples in the Americas; fat-tailed sheep and sorghum in South Africa. Ultimately, however, the interconnected scientific knowledge and technical advances of colonizing communities, capitalist enterprises and government agencies were the main motors of transformation. Frontiers of agriculture were multifaceted – often shaped by the particular commercial commodity which dragged or pushed them forward. In both southern Africa and North America, far-flung grazing frontiers expanded alongside more all-embracing transplantations akin to those of Eurasia. In the northern coastal states of North America, a mixed imported agriculture, essentially grain-based, prevailed from early on as it did in the western Cape. By the end of the eighteenth century, these systems both fed local markets and yielded surplus for export, such as wine from the Cape and cattle from New England. Australia-bound emigrant ships also stopped at the Cape to pick up livestock, launching the Australian stock industry.

Especially during the earlier, more subsistence-oriented phases, settler farming was characterized by a diversified husbandry that brought in the new without entirely banishing the old. Oaks and vines may have been prominent symbols of colonization at the Cape but were merely interspersed among the broad mountain swathes of fynbos. And beyond the meadows, vegetable plot, orchard, barnyard and woodlot of the typical eighteenth-century New England farmstead lay a forested zone that provided berries and game. Merchant (1989: 149, 116) points out that these agriculturalists, accepted nature as an animate being to be 'wooed' and 'nursed'.

By contrast, the plantation system that enveloped the Caribbean and the southern reaches of mainland North America involved a more wholesale takeover. This originally Mediterranean capitalist form matured outside Europe, not least on Atlantic islands, and reached its apogee in the Americas from the early seventeenth century. While South African settlers imported slaves, the plantation system there spread largely after abolition. Until the advent of railways, plantations clung to colonial coasts and rivers in order to face outward to the world economy for which they were producing vital new commodities. It was only by water, whether sea or river, that bulky exports could be carried profitably. As capital-intensive undertakings they required relatively little land in relation to the value they produced. But they were totally new social forms, which thoroughly transformed their host environments through the clearing of vegetation, intensive production and processing. Where sugar, cotton, tobacco, indigo and rice ruled, whether on small island or mainland, there forests and swamplands disappeared and soil served the crop until it was exhausted. The plantation crops grown to satisfy newly created consumption needs, not least a growing European sweet tooth, could not be produced in temperate climes. By definition they were established in tropical and sub-tropical zones which were often home to a rich variety of plants and animals.

The ecological drawbacks of monoculture were quickly apparent. Tropical soils were often relatively poor, their poverty temporarily disguised by a rich layer of rotting vegetable matter derived from a dense forest cover. Once cleared, extensive hoeing and weeding exposed soil to the elements, while rigid planted rows invited erosion by producing ideal channels for runoff. Single-crop concentration largely precluded rotation. American settlers abandoned the indigenous practice of mixed cropping with corn in a single field. Though they replaced this with rotation to some extent, the most common sequence was for corn to follow tobacco, both injurious to the soil. Within a few cycles, land was often abandoned, as 'sour lands', to tree encroachment. The shortage of livestock diminished the supply of barnyard fertilizer. Guano scraped from the rocks of South America, transported long and tortuous routes by sea (which might add a third to the cost), fed the soils of wealthier planters, especially during the 'guano mania' of the 1840s and 1850s. Monoculture also hastened the build-up of soil toxins and parasites; a nation that shrewdly built an elaborate system of checks and balances into its political system was completely neglectful of the same when it came to its agricultural constitution.

Concern about deforestation and soil exhaustion was manifest on Caribbean plantation islands and American coastal strips in the eighteenth century. Gentlemen farmers such as George Washington and Thomas Jefferson dabbled with enlightened husbandry on their estates, experimenting with deeper ploughing, gully filling and the use of animal and plant fertilizer. Plantation soil exhaustion became part of the debate about the efficiency and benefits of slave production, and the system's appetite for fresh soil fuelled the territorial expansion of the southern plantation economy as far west as eastern Texas. The sharecropping and wage labour that had replaced slavery by the late nineteenth century were no less greedy, and environmental impacts actually peaked after the Civil War (1861–5). As the future 'father of soil conservation', H.H. Bennett, was growing up on a North Carolina cotton plantation surrounded by the problems of erosion, the cotton belt was seen as thoroughly mined.

Similarly, the heyday of sugar is often associated with slavery, yet it was only after abolition in the British empire (1834) that British consumption really took off and a renewed push began into the tropical zones. Consumption in the United Kingdom rose from 19 lbs a head per year in 1830 to 71 per head in 1890. (Richardson, 1986: 129). American per capita consumption in 1887 was 61 lbs – second only to British (Mintz, 1985: 188). Natal, along with Queensland, Fiji, Hawaii and Trinidad, became a major sugar zone during this post-slavery phase. In place of the lush and diverse sub-tropical coastal bush and forests, with dense cover of strelitzia (wild banana) and ilala palm, the landscape was ever more one of monolithic greenswards of sugar with blotches of cultivated banana and wattle.

Beyond intensive early colonial coast-bound agriculture, grazing drove a mobile, expansive and plundering frontier forward. In both regions, sheep were its shock troops. The trekboer economy in the first two centuries of South African settlement always faced partly in the direction of coastal trading centres because it depended on the exchange of animals and their products for guns, ammunition, horses, wagons and metal goods, not to mention coffee, which were essential to colonial expansion. Until the 1820s its markets were primarily for meat on the coast, and the animals, long before the era of refrigeration, had to get there live. This put enormous pressure on the droving routes to and from Cape Town. As a result, areas were reserved as public property along the routes where the cattle and sheep could rest and feed. These were called *uitspanne* in Afrikaans or outspans in English – the word for taking the team of oxen out of the yoke that later became associated with oranges and relaxation. As long as markets primarily required meat, it was not essential to dispense with the hairy (non-woolled), fat-tailed sheep long run by the Khoikhoi.

It was largely the British settlement in the eastern Cape, new trading ports and, more than anything else, woolled Merino sheep from Spain, that transformed the grazing frontier in the second half of the nineteenth century. These sheep adapted well to the sparse grazing and long treks of the semi-arid interior of the Karoo. Wool was South Africa's major agricultural export as early as 1840; it remained so to 1930 when sheep numbers swelled to nearly 45 million. This rivalled numbers in the United States – which peaked at 52 million in the early 1880s – though the latter region had a far larger grazing area.

American settler sheep (also mostly Merino) superseded an older Spanish ranchero and Native American sheep culture based on the coarser-woolled Churro breed (the native bighorn sheep was never domesticated). During the 1840s, sheep flocked out of their original northeastern settler stronghold on to the humid prairies of Illinois and Wisconsin. The major pre-Civil War growth area, however, was the semi-arid Southwest. In California, to feed hungry miners, numbers rose from 20,000 to a million between 1850 and 1860. Civil War demand for uniforms stimulated further spread. In the wake of the collapse of the Great Plains cattle industry in the 1880s, the sheep frontier did a U-turn and moved east to colonize these vacated areas.

Sheep enjoyed a number of advantages for frontier farmers: a small initial capital outlay, a quick cash income in easily stored and transported wool as well as a market for meat, their more modest thirst, their ability to graze high and poor terrain, and their manageability. Yet despite the sheer numbers involved and the epic sheep drives, historians of the American West have largely ignored them in favour of cattle – reflecting the nineteenth-century rancher's prejudice against 'woollies' and the unmounted, often non-Anglo-Saxon sheepmen. In fact, sheep and cattle were sometimes grazed together.

Cattle were lodged at the heart of African economic and cultural life in South Africa. Up to 1930, Africans still owned half the cattle despite the fact that over 75 per cent of the country constituted settler farms. The switch by indigenous people from hoe to ox-drawn plough agriculture reinforced the centrality of 'the god with the moist nose' (Guy, 1987: 18). Settlers adopted much of the African cattle complex but, authorized not least by their Calvinist gods, turned it into a much more hard-nosed commercial enterprise. Most pioneer homesteads in eastern America included a few head of cattle (providing manure for grain among other things) and poorer upland soils were regularly used for pasture. But the Great Plains represented a huge natural pasture, and discussion of cattle in US history is essentially tied to the cattle kingdom that emerged there after the Civil War.

Bison-replacing cattle served domestic markets that were far larger in the United States than in South Africa – where the bulk of the African population had their own supplies. Chicago in particular, 'the great bovine city of the world' (Cronon, 1991: 207), became head of rail processing and redistributing centre for herds of beasts which had in turn tramped, eaten and then transformed the prairie grasses. Railways linking Chicago to points west furnished access to a vast hinterland largely devoid of navigable rivers and inhospitable for crop raising, while the eastern spokes of the hub enabled the city to serve the nation's major urban meat markets.

Livestock were the mainstay of inland settlers in South Africa until the 1910s. The turn to systematic grain production – the great highveld maize revolution – was effected by established communities of Africans and Boers facing and grasping a fresh opportunity as the gold-mining Mecca of the Witwatersrand boomed. Large-scale grain production was more quickly taken up on the more varied and commercially vibrant US frontier. Railways and machinery brought new crop-growing settlers to the rich lands south and west of Chicago, which proved hospitable to the familiar maize, soft wheats and hogs. By the 1880s, encouraged by a spell of unusually abundant rain, small farmers were moving *en masse* on to the more arid plains. Cattle barons, who had made quick money by accumulating huge numbers that fattened for free on the unfenced public domain, had already suffered catastrophic losses from drought, severe winters and pasture exhaustion. Whereas South Africa had little over 600,000 white settlers in all around 1890, the American plains alone accounted for over 6 million.

In the United States the strength of the market enabled farmers in better watered states close to rail centres, such as Iowa, to grow crops as animal feed. Corn, especially, which fattened animals more quickly, was converted into tender beef and pork. This helped save the pastures though it brought even larger areas under the plough. In most of South Africa, however, and in the more distant ranching states of the United States, farmers continued to depend on the natural grazing. Colonization drew new civil authority and technology into the South African interior and the trans-Mississippi West. In the vanguard of penetration after the Civil War, alongside cattle, sheep and hogs, were the sheriff's and magistrate's offices, lock-up, saloon, barbed wire, steel plough and firearms. Water provision was vital for effective stock farming and borehole technology powered by steel windmills extended the carrying capacity in the sub-humid interiors.

In South Africa, a roving, relatively independent transhumant grazing and hunting culture, moulded by periodic and seasonal drought, persisted longer than its American counterpart where the 'big man' backed by 'big capital' took control sooner and more emphatically. A mobile black tenantry also with their own stock survived well into the interwar years. This life on trek (which also involved bringing stock to market) was later remembered by Boers with the same affection as cowboy life in the American West. Yet in the absence of so powerful a myth-making industry, it was not romanticized for consumption as a defining national self-image. In actuality, the late nineteenth-century American cowboy was more wage worker than backwoods frontiersman – and often black or Hispanic to boot. In both countries, however, memories of this era were 'whitened', though recent postmodern westerns like *Posse* have attempted tentative recolourings.

Frontier settlement is often regarded as part of an eleutherian flight from industry and the influence of mining also sits ill with the agrarian ideal. Ghost towns of the Mother Lode in California and the Barberton region of the eastern Transvaal may seem quaint today but at their height they were as harsh and environmentally dismal as any nineteenth-century industrial region. Mining, belying the picturesque image of 'mom and pop' pick, shovel and pan operation, was in fact the grinding edge of industrial and urban intrusion in many unsettled frontier regions. By the 1880s, over 50 per cent of Cape exports were diamonds. And within fifteen years of their discovery, Kimberley was second only to Cape Town as South Africa's largest urban settlement. Its Big Hole (wider than the Mississippi) is now a tourist attraction but the 'blue' diamondiferous soil had to be gouged out of the veld. Butte, Montana, lay at the heart of the American West's black country, a wasteland of sterile slag dumps. Emissions from smelter stacks killed off all vegetation for miles, poisoning cattle and their forage with arsenic. In 1898, one Butte copper king built a $1 million amusement park nearby. Columbia Gardens, just beyond the atmospheric death zone, featured a huge bed of some 85,000 pansies – the only living flowers around; the children of what constituted an industrial proletariat grimy as any were graciously allowed to pick them (Bartlett, 1974: 265–6).

Miners upstream required tremendous quantities of water for working and processing ore. In the nineteenth-century American West, the English common law notion of equal access for all owners of lands adjacent to water was replaced by the doctrine of first use, which might involve complete appropriation. This thirsty industry deprived farmers and growing numbers of urban consumers downriver. There was no hydraulic mining in southern Africa but in the American West from the early 1850s jets of water spurting out of the nozzles of cannon at high pressure reduced hillsides to slurry that flushed into the sluices: 'boulders two feet thick were washed and batted down like so many marbles' (Bartlett, 1974: 269). In California tailings raised the level of stream beds dramatically which, despite levee construction, flooded fields and orchards downstream with turgid water polluted by heavy metals. Only in the 1880s, when agriculture had outstripped gold mining in economic importance to the state did politicians act to outlaw hydraulicking.

Politicians were now intervening not only to safeguard agrarian interests but to facilitate their expansion. The US Department of Agriculture (1862) and its Cape counterpart, founded some twenty years later, were both initially concerned with scientific research and education designed, in American parlance, to 'make two blades of grass grow where one grew before'. American strategy took shape around the Land Grant colleges that promoted the mechanical and agricultural arts (1862), the experimentation stations located at these colleges (1887), and the federal extension service (1914). In South Africa, the control of diseases, themselves often intimately bound up with changing environmental conditions, preoccupied the early agricultural bureaucracy. The country was plagued only at its margins with tropical diseases such as trypanosomiasis (tsetse fly). Introduced diseases, such as phylloxera which swept through vineyards worldwide in the 1880s, proved more lethal. (By the turn of the century, new root stocks had been imported from California.) Subsequently, scab in sheep, rinderpest and east coast fever in cattle seemed to threaten the future of agriculture; their control enabled rapid increase in stocking levels and production.

The study of plant and animal diseases was also a formative function of US authorities. Their broad-fronted assault targeted locusts in the West and disease-bearing ticks that were frustrating late nineteenth-century efforts to diversify the South's economy by building up a stock industry. The crusade against the Mexican boll weevil which began a remorseless eastward expansion in 1894 truly mobilized federal funds and expertise. The demoralizing fight against the weevil played a large part in getting US government entomologists into the insecticide habit – an approach that was eventually resorted to against the ill-understood tsetse in South Africa.

THE CONSERVATIONIST STATE

Even before cattle baron gave way to sod-buster in the late nineteenth-century American West, a minority of federal government officials, notably John Wesley Powell, chief of the US Geological Survey, were aware of the potential environmental consequences of attempts to raise the same humid zone crops in a land of little rain. In his seminal *Report on the Lands of the Arid Region of the United States* (1878), Powell stressed the inhibiting role of the environment and recommended a large-unit ranching economy over traditional homesteading for much of the unsettled West. Such warnings, however, fell on stony ground for they flew in the face of government policy and public optimism about the prospects for arable farming in the West.

From very early on in the history of settler farming in South Africa, there were complaints of overstocking. In 1775, the Swedish traveller Sparrman noted 'the grasses and herbs which these animals most covet are prevented continually more and more from thriving and taking root, while on the contrary the rhinoceros bush which the cattle always leave untouched is suffered to take root free and unmolested' (Hall, 1934: 67). On the American high plains, inedible, hard-stemmed ironweed, rolling tumbleweed (actually a Russian immigrant) and prickly pear spread to displace more palatable grasses. Stock liked the grassy vleis or shallow depressions around watercourses and played a major part in destroying these, ousting wildlife.

In defining the problems South African officials drew on their knowledge of Europe, India and Australia but especially of the United States under the presidency of Theodore Roosevelt (1901–9), who spearheaded the American conservation offensive. The federal pro-gramme focused primarily on public lands, but those who were seen to be misusing their private resources also came under attack. Conserva-tionism gained strength from the conviction – bolstered by the formal announcement of the closing of the frontier in 1890 – that settlers could no longer mine the land and move on.

Soil erosion from overgrazing rather than cultivation was pinpointed as the South African malaise. The scarcity of water sources in the Karoo and the highveld grasslands entailed daily movements of stock. Few farmers were prepared to leave their animals far from their farmstead enclosures (kraals) because of the threat of theft and predators and it became a commonplace observation that 'flocks tramp out more than they eat' (Drought Investigation Commission, 1922: 14).

In South Africa, the most effective sheep predator was the jackal. As in the United States, stockmen constantly clamoured for extermination of these 'vermin'. However, high bounties were only imposed on jackals and feline predators such as caracals when officials came to see them as indirectly responsible for wearing out the veld as well as consuming unacceptable amounts of lamb. In five years during the late 1910s and early 1920s, over 300,000 pelts were brought in for reward in the Cape alone. At the behest of western stockmen's associations – whose political clout matched the environmental impact of their animals – the US Congress in 1915 began funding predator 'control'. As in South Africa, the annual body count in the United States (at about 35,000) seems to have peaked in the years immediately after the First World War. The farmer – and in the United States his ally the government predator control agent – is unlikely to supersede the hunter as archsymbol of wildlife destruction. But those distributing a quarter horse carcass laced with cyanide or strychnine are legitimate quarry for the environmental historian. Poison and traps were (and remain) less discriminating than gunshot, leading to a host of secondary killings.

Conservationists welcomed the eradication of jackals as they felt it would open the way to more rational use of pastures with rotatable fenced paddocks in which animals could be left overnight. 'Conservation' in this context was very much associated with the American priority of efficient resource use to maximize commercial production, rather than with retaining a diversity of species on farmland. Vermin remained a wide category and the process of rehabilitation in human eyes was long and fraught for any given species.

The guiding principle of soil conservation was expressed in lay terms by a Texas sheep-herder: 'Grass is what counts. It's what saves us all – far as we get saved. . . . Grass is what holds the earth together' (Worster, 1979: 78). Such views informed the deliberations of the South African Drought Commission (1922–3) whose conservationist language pervaded the region's debate for decades. Two of the Afrikaner members of the Commission had trained or worked in the United States as refugees after the South African War (1899–1902). H.S.D. du Toit, its chairman, trained there as an agronomist; he later became head of South Africa's agricultural extension service. R.J. van Reenen studied civil engineering and worked on irrigation projects in Nebraska before returning to the Transvaal civil service. T.D. Hall, one of the first South Africans to write systematic historical studies of pastures, studied agriculture in Illinois in the 1910s.

In the United States, soil erosion investigations on a national basis first received Congressional funding in the late 1920s. Stress was laid not only on the dangers of gulley erosion (dongas) – where concentrated streams of water dug deep into the soil – but also on the more insidious process of sheet erosion or soil washing. H.H. Bennett's favourite lobbying device was to spread a bath towel on a tilted table and pour water on it from a pitcher, to demonstrate how water could be absorbed. He would then remove the towel and pour water over the bare surface, which proceeded to run off as it would on land stripped of vegetative cover (Brink, 1951: 18). Techniques of control were developed for cultivated lands, such as grass strips between fields and ridges (or bunds) thrown up along the contour at regular intervals, on sloping land. Ploughing along the contour became the extension officer's battlecry. Drawing on European and Russian experience, South African officials subsidized the planting of windbreaks, mostly exotic gums and pines (see chapter 3), around fields in flat highveld districts. On the American plains, there was relatively little windbreak planting until Franklin D. Roosevelt's programmes during the 1930s. Water runoff was the main source of erosion across both countries but it was the winds that scoured out the Dust Bowl which whipped up American attention.

While South African environmental problems were primarily caused by overgrazing, the American Dust Bowl was more closely related to cropping than stocking. Indeed, overlooking their own capacity to inflict damage, American ranchers argued that the disaster could have been avoided if the area had been left to grass for cattle. Early mechanization (tractors, trucks and combine harvesters replacing oxen and horses) was also a far more potent factor in American soil erosion. Ford alone had sold 650,000 tractors before 1930 when there were barely 4,000 in South Africa. To some degree, South Africa was saved from a worse ecological disaster in the 1930s by shortage of capital and machinery, as well as by the cheapness of tenant labour. In America, dry farming techniques using new moldboard ploughs exposed earth on a far wider scale than hitherto possible. John Steinbeck evoked its effect in *The Grapes of Wrath* (1939: 417) by writing of 'surgery' rather than ploughing.

International demand, stimulated by the First World War, propelled prices upwards through the 1910s. As production expanded in areas such as the Soviet Union and Argentina in the 1920s, prices – as yet largely unregulated by governments – became increasingly volatile and went into decline. In both regions, farmers attempted to compensate for unstable, falling prices, and rising debt, by producing more – with devastating environmental effects. Grass was eaten lower, tramped harder ('hammered' to use the South African expression) and marginal fragile soils ploughed up. While prices were falling, wool production increased in South Africa from 185 million lbs in 1925 to 297 million in 1933/4 – in the United States from 292 to 460 million.

The impact of the ensuing Great Depression was exacerbated by drought as well as by swarming plagues of voracious locusts, always menacing during such cycles. In part, drought was caused by a reduction in the denuded earth's capacity to absorb and store water but these were unusually dry years within longer-term rainfall cycles. Many American states, especially on the southern plains, suffered their lowest recorded rainfall: 1934 appears to have been the driest year in both countries (though in the US 1935 was the worst for dust storms, and 1936 brought the hottest and coldest temperatures since records began).

The regulation of agriculture had lost ground during the 1910s and 1920s, when conservation in general had become too closely associated with federal power. Thanks to the American Dust Bowl, it regained centre stage. The conservationist agenda was interlinked with the plethora of interventionist New Deal programmes, especially with the idea of government-planned land use – a more alien notion in the US than it was in a former colony with a firmer tradition of authoritarian central control. The Soil Erosion Service (1933), its successor the Soil Conservation Service (1935), and the Taylor Grazing Act (1934) emerged from this linkage, plugging technocratic solutions. The latter act withdrew from settlement all remaining public lands, many of them under grass, ending a timehonoured federal policy of public domain disposal into private hands. This was not a dramatic turnabout, however, as these lands were divided into grazing districts with modest user fees. The most evangelical campaigner for state intervention, H.H. Bennett, possessed an immaculate sense of timing. While congressmen debated the merits of his soil conservation proposals in 1935 Bennett contrived to detain them until the moment that anticipated dust storms blew prime topsoil into the committee rooms of Washington, D.C.: 'This gentlemen, is what I have been talking about!' he exclaimed, gesturing toward the nearest window (Worster, 1979: 213).

By the late 1920s, officials in South Africa had called a national conference and made conservation part of the agricultural extension programme. The Soil Erosion Act of 1932 provided large funds for conservation and water works on farms. A sub-department of soil and veld conservation was subsequently set up within the Department of Agriculture. Bennett's tour of southern Africa in 1944 served as a major propaganda exercise for the South African agricultural bureaucracy. Bringing with him what his biographer refers to as 'the immense prestige of American accomplishment', Bennett stumped the country lamenting what he considered the modest record of the South African government and advocating the adoption of American-style soil conservation districts (Brink, 1951: 138–9). These were to some extent realized in the South African Soil Conservation Act of 1946 which created largely self-regulating local soil conservation committees. Though officials suggested compulsory measures, politicians were hesitant to introduce them for white farmers, despite the precedents set in the eradication of scab from sheep, and of east coast fever from cattle. In practice, it proved very difficult for farmers to act against one of their peers and in general the committees relied on education and exhortation.

In the United States, the federal government did buy up some bankrupt land, from which environmental benefits did accrue: Shenandoah national park in the Appalachians, enlarged Indian reservations, new wildlife refuges and grasslands in the heart of the Dust Bowl. Grasslands (amounting to an area the size of Maryland) were first acquired under emergency sub-marginal land-acquisition programmes and replaced cropping with grazing stock and wildlife. Operating under the 1913 and 1936 Natives Land and Trust Acts, the South African government purchased smaller areas of land largely for the purposes of extending African reserves. All new African settlements on these Trust lands were subject to rigid planning controls. Attempts were also made to protect watersheds around the sources of major eastward flowing rivers such as the Tugela.

Conservation policy from the 1910s to the 1950s, dominated by the language of efficiency, was often unfriendly to small frontier farmers and more particularly tenant farmers. Legislation and the rise of large-scale commercial grain farming in South Africa had undermined African sharecropping on white land. Black sharecroppers in the American South were quitting their tenancies for northern ghettos and factories, hounded out as much by the tractor as Jim Crow segregationist laws. South African farmers feared infection of their herds and flocks by tenants' stock and used the same metaphors of contagion that justified segregation of people in town. Controls over fire, fencing, disease and transhumance, partly justified by conservationist imperatives, worked against smallholding tenants. Given the conditions under which many sharecroppers operated – they had to maximize production in a short space of time, under constant threat of eviction – their farming practices may have been environmentally damaging.

If the segregationist South African state was cautious in its dealings with white farmers, it adopted a more directive approach toward African agriculture in the reserves (later homelands). About 40 per cent of African people lived within the boundaries of these areas, legislatively designated for their exclusive occupation, and bursting at the seams. White fears of being swamped by rapid African urbanization spawned by perceived environmental collapse added urgency to government intervention. A scheme for the betterment of the African reserves was proclaimed in 1939. State officials would plan each area individually, demarcating arable, grazing, residential land and woodlots. Scattered African settlements would be concentrated in villages and pastures fenced in camps along the lines advocated for large white farms. This was an enormously ambitious programme and only small beginnings were made prior to the 1950s. Yet it remained at the core of state policy for half a century (see chapter 6).

In the early nineteenth century, the entire 'uninhabitable' area west of the Mississippi was designated as Indian Territory, to which remnant eastern tribes such as the Cherokee were removed. When even these lands eventually proved enticing to whites, Indian lands were more meagrely specified and occupants became wards of their federal guardian. Reservations, the equivalent of the South African homelands, were also subject to heavy-handed reform policies – yet with little more success. The controversy over grazing on the Navajo reservation serves as a vivid case study. An enriched pastoralist culture had emerged as the Navajo adopted sheep and goats. After American conquest in the 1860s, they resumed pastoralism within a reservation and their numbers rose steadily from some 8,000 to around 50,000 by the 1930s. This was accompanied by a surge in grazing animals from some 30,000 to 1.37 million head over the same period. Restricted as they were to an elevated area that seldom received over ten inches of precipitation, and penned in by expanding white flocks, the result was acute overgrazing and attendant soil erosion.

As in southern Africa, livestock became concentrated around water supplies. The Navajo also corralled (kraaled) their sheep to protect them from coyotes, exacerbating uneven use of the range. Just as in South Africa, where African farmers were blamed for erosion, federal conservationists placed responsibility for this particular part of the Dust Bowl squarely on the Navajo. The technocratic solution in both countries involved stock reduction and improvement through better sires, and elimination of commercially useless animals such as goats and horses – all of which disregarded the wider role of stock within tribal culture as sources of food, milk, work and prestige (the latter based on quantity rather than quality). What appears to have given the conservationist argument extra clout in the 1930s was the imperative of preventing the world's largest and most expensive water development project, Hoover Dam, from silting up. According to the experts, much of the silt suspended in the Colorado river drained from the Navajo reservation. Protection of dam watersheds was often cited as urgent justification for betterment or land rehabilitation on African reserves. Navajo livestock were culled by over a half between 1933 and 1946. The Navajo solution, however, was more land and their hostility to this form of transnational conservation logic paralleled that of their African counterparts who had been the target of similar policies.

Antagonisms on the Navajo reservation eased off with the return of above average rainfall during and after the Second World War. The return of the rains throughout our regions was matched by the rise of agricultural prices and farm production boomed again, assisted by fertilizers and the tapping of deeper water supplies. The ecological disasters of the 1930s had not precluded buoyant recovery in which the sceptics were shouldered aside to be left muttering that judgment day had merely been postponed. In the mid-1950s a dry spell returned to the US plains but a full-scale reprise of the 'dirty thirties' was staved off partly by the availability of underground water, and the region continued to function as the 'breadbasket of the world'.

The tensions between increasing production and environmental constraints can be illustrated by developments in the eastern Orange Free State (OFS), a highveld region with about 25 inches of rainfall that is more akin to the higher altitude northern plains of the US than to the classic Dust Bowl region further south. In 1948, the Kipling-quoting British colonial, Sam Bairstow, together with a few enamoured farmers, directly adapted American dryland (moisture-conserving) techniques for wheat on land hitherto relatively marginal for crops. They followed the system which had contributed to the US Dust Bowl of the 1930s – a long clean fallow that allowed the land to absorb water over a full year without any grass or weed cover to use it. Within a decade, the experiment proved so successful – coinciding as it did with a period of high prices and rapid mechanization – that large areas of surrounding veld were ploughed up with newly introduced machinery, some of it American.

Farmers inaugurated a phase of wheat monocropping that helped keep South Africa self-sufficient in this crop at a time when urbanizing blacks were switching from maize porridge to bread. Despite systems of ridge terracing, the possibility of environmental trouble lurked. Potential difficulties were averted by unexpected quirks of nature: new insect pests (Russian aphid) and weeds demanded systems of rotation with sunflower and maize and more varied fallows which helped cover the bare ground. When costs (not least for fuel) increased from the 1970s, more marginal land was taken out of cultivation, as it was on the US Great Plains. By the 1980s, state subsidization of planted pastures with native species of grass further diversified the fields.

Smaller areas of land were able to produce the same crop. The OFS wheat bonanza squandered the fragile topsoil in some districts but a combination of unpredictable pressures rescued the bulk of the soil.

In both post-war South Africa and the United States, the application of generous doses of chemical fertilizer (see chapter 6) and water enhanced agricultural output. Water is the critical natural resource for sustaining life in all forms across large parts of our regions. The problem of water shortage (and storage) is compounded by the sporadic nature of most rain – much of it falling during summer storms with rapid runoff. The harnessing of water in dams and ditches on a large scale became indispensable to commercial farming. By 1980, South Africa was devoting 75 per cent of its piped water to agriculture, a higher proportion than most other countries, including the United States with around 50 per cent. Only in California, the pivot of agribusiness, did the figure go higher than South Africa's. Despite the fierce anti-centralist stance of farm lobbies with their Jeffersonian yeoman rhetoric, their sights were firmly set on the federal government largesse slopping out of the bulging reclamation pork barrel. A fraternity of zealous experts organized within the US Army Corps of Engineers marched up river valleys throwing up dams, their monumental structures made possible by new methods of steel and concrete construction. In South Africa, large dams, also named after leading politicians, epitomized the Nationalist party approach to agricultural development. The H.F. Verwoerd Dam, raised on the Orange River in the 1970s, sent water hundreds of kilometres through what was hailed as one of the longest underground tunnels in the world to the fruit and grain producing valleys of the eastern Cape.

Irrigation served white rather than black farmers in South Africa and was the cockpit of conflict between urban use/agribusiness and small-scale Hispanic farmers in the American southwest.[1] In the boom era for dam building in South Africa, the Jozini Dam at the Pongola Gorge on the edge of sub-tropical Maputaland, designed to irrigate 'poor white' sugar farms in northeastern Natal, subjected African floodplain farming to unsuitably long periods of inundation (Ramphele, 1991: 67). In the American West, agriculture's thirst was rivalled by that of the urban (and increasingly suburban) consumer. Some of the water in southern Californian swimming pools and domestic showers begins life as snow in the Rockies. These manipulations have turned the desert southwest into the sunbelt's hottest property, a leading area of post-1945 demographic and economic growth. Witwatersrand consumer demand has stretched water supplies on the highveld but the conflict between farmer and urbanite here is only beginning, as individual houses in the burgeoning black locations (townships sited far from major urban centres) are now slowly being hooked up to the mains water supply. A position more pregnant with implications for the future is the fundamental objection to wild habitat consuming large dams which flood canyons and reduce raging waters to a trickle. For many modern environmentalists, the dam has come to symbolize the dubious thrust of technocratic conservation, now recast as the antithesis of environmentalism (see chapter 6).

The commercialized colonial agricultures that spread to cover the great bulk of South Africa and the USA did contain immense destructive tendencies. It is doubtful whether the 'old' world could be restored. Perhaps twentieth-century agrarian systems are nowhere 'sustainable' even within the transformed natural world created to accommodate them. But ecological outcomes remain unpredictable. Where fields have been abandoned over the centuries for residential growth, ecological systems, though by no means restored, can become more varied (and leafy) through sensitive incorporation of green spaces. In some areas where wilderness is long gone, environments simplified by agriculture have spawned an alternative rural aesthetic which, as in Europe with its hedgerows, flower-studded meadows and spinneys, is thought of and cherished as 'nature', however carefully managed and manicured. After decades of hand-wringing, a handful of optimistic botanists is beginning to conclude that the natural veld in the Karoo is improving; one cause may be a reduction in sheep numbers due to low wool prices. And after farmers quit the thin, stony soils of New England for richer western prairies, secondary forest soon recolonized and one often stumbles upon a tumbled-down dry stone wall when walking in the woods.

NOTE

1 Robert Redford's film, *The Milagro Bean Field Wars* (1988), centres on the struggle between Hispanic farmers of this type and a recent adjacent recreation complex that threatens to divert 'their' water to keep the golf greens green for well-heeled white visitors.

REFERENCES AND FURTHER READING

Bartlett, Richard (1974) *The New Country: A Social History of the American Frontier, 1776–1890*, New York: Oxford University Press.

Beinart, William (1982) *The Political Economy of Pondoland 1860–1930*, Cambridge: Cambridge University Press.

—— (1984) 'Soil erosion, conservationism and ideas about development: a southern African exploration, 1900–1960', *Journal of Southern African Studies*, 11 (1), 52–83.

—— (1989) 'Introduction: The politics of colonial conservation', *Journal of Southern African Studies*, 15 (2), 143–62.

—— (1993) 'La nuit du chacal: moutons, pâturages et prédateurs en Afrique du Sud de 1900 à 1930' ('The night of the jackal: sheep, predators and pastures in South Africa'), *Revue Français d'Histoire d'Outre-mer*, LXXX (298), 105–29.

Brink, Wellington (1951) *Big Hugh: The Father of Soil Conservation*, New York: Macmillan.

Bundy, Colin (1979) *The Rise and Fall of the South African Peasantry*, London: Heinemann.

Cowdrey, Albert E. (1983) *This Land, This South: An Environmental History*, Lexington: University Press of Kentucky.

Cronon, William (1991) *Nature's Metropolis: Chicago and the Great West*, New York: W.W. Norton.

—— (1992) 'A place for stories: nature, history and narrative', *Journal of American History*, 78 (March), 1347–76.

Crosby, Alfred (1986) *Ecological Imperialism*, New York: Cambridge University Press.

Davenport, T.R.H. (1966) *The Afrikaner Bond*, Cape Town: Oxford University Press.

Dickinson, E.B. (1978) 'Wheat development in the Orange Free State: some recollections', *Fertilizer Society of South Africa Journal*, 2, 73–8.

Drought Investigation Commission, Union of South Africa (1922) *Interim Report* (U.G.70).

—— (1923) *Final Report* (U.G.49).

Dunlap, Thomas R. (1988) *Saving America's Wildlife: Ecology and the American Mind, 1850–1990*, Princeton: Princeton University Press.

El-Ashry, Mohamed T. and Gibbons, Diana C. (eds) (1988) *Water and Arid Lands of the Western United States*, Cambridge: Cambridge University Press.

Fonaroff, L. Schuyler (1963) 'Conservation and stock reduction on the Navajo tribal range', *Geographical Review*, LIII (2), 200–23.

Ford, J. (1971) *The Role of Trypanosomiasis in African Ecology: A Study of the Tsetse Fly Problem*, Oxford: Oxford University Press.

Genovese, Eugene D. (1961) *The Political Economy of Slavery: Studies in the Economy and Society of the Slave South*, New York: Random House.

Guy, J. (1987) 'Analysing pre-capitalist societies in southern Africa', *Journal of Southern African Studies*, 14 (1), 18–37.

Hall, T.D. (1934) 'South African pastures: retrospective and prospective', *South African Journal of Science*, 31, 59–97.

—— (1942) *Our Veld: A Major National Problem*, Johannesburg (pamphlet).

Hoffman, M.T. and Cowling, Richard (1990) 'Vegetation change in the semi-arid eastern Karoo over the last 200 years – fact or fiction?', *South African Journal of Science*, 86, 286–94.

Jacks, G.V. and Whyte, R.O. (1939) *The Rape of the Earth: A World Survey of Soil Erosion*, London: Faber & Faber.

Jordan, A.M. (1986) *Trypanosomiasis Control and African Rural Development*, Oxford: Oxford University Press.

Kolodny, Annette (1984) *The Land before Her: Fantasy and Experience of the*

American Frontiers 1630–1860, Chapel Hill: University of North Carolina Press.

Landau, Paul S. (1993) 'When rain falls: rainmaking and community in a Tswana village, *c.*1870 to recent times', *International Journal of African Historical Studies*, 26 (1), 1–30.

Malin, James C. (1947) *The Grasslands of North America: Prolegomena to its History*, Lawrence: privately published.

Merchant, Carolyn (1989) *Ecological Revolutions: Nature, Gender and Science in New England*, Chapel Hill: University of North Carolina Press.

Mintz, Sidney W. (1985) *Sweetness and Power: The Place of Sugar in Modern History*, New York: Penguin.

Opie, John (1987) *The Law of the Land: Two Hundred Years of American Farmland Policy*, Lincoln: University of Nebraska Press.

Ramphele, Mamphela (ed.) (1991) *Restoring the Land: Environment and Change in Post-Apartheid South Africa*, London: Panos.

Richardson, Peter (1986) 'The Natal sugar industry in the nineteenth century', in W. Beinart, Peter Delius and Stanley Trapido (eds), *Putting a Plough to the Ground: Accumulation and Dispossession in Rural South Africa 1850–1930*, Johannesburg: Ravan Press.

Ryder, M.L. (1983) *Sheep and Man*, London: Duckworth.

Sears, Paul B. (1939) *Deserts on the March*, Norman: University of Oklahoma Press.

Steinbeck, John (1939) *The Grapes of Wrath*, New York: Heinemann.

Union of South Africa, Province of the Cape of Good Hope (1924), *First and Second Reports of the Vermin Extermination Commission* (C.P. 3).

Van der Merwe, N.J. (1953) 'The jackal', *Flora and Fauna*, 4, 1–82.

Webb, Walter P. (1931) *The Great Plains*, Boston: Ginn.

Worster, Donald (1979) *Dust Bowl: The Southern Plains in the 1930s*, New York: Oxford University Press.

—— (1985) *Rivers of Empire: Water, Aridity and the Growth of the American West*, New York: Pantheon.

—— (1992) *Under Western Skies: Nature and History in the American West*, New York: Oxford University Press.

Worster, Donald, Crosby, A., White, R., Merchant, C. and Cronon, W. (1990) 'A roundtable: environmental history', *Journal of American History*, 76 (March), 1078–106.

5 Nature reserves and national parks: revaluing and renaturing the wild

National parks are emblematic of conservation as a venture in the mind of many white Americans and South Africans. Their protagonists perceive and present them as its purest and most altruistic expression. Yet game reserves, national parks and similar wilderness areas are systematically and sometimes intensively managed spaces subject to a wide variety of crosscutting interests. Many blacks in both countries have seen them as exclusive spaces catering to the cultural and recreational tastes of the monied and mobile middle classes. Historical analysis of these areas must begin with these recognitions. Moreover, the very idea of wilderness, as we have emphasized, is a cultural construct rather than a precise physical entity. God, according to an American aphorism, may have created the world, but only Congress can create wilderness. While ecological interrelationships have their own dynamics, the leeway given to nature is increasingly shaped by human intervention.

PRESERVATION, TOURISM AND DEPICTIONS OF NATURE

The areas involved are not vast. In the United States (excluding Alaska), only 1.75 per cent of the land is reserved as National Park; the South African figure is higher at about 3 per cent. In other parts of our subcontinents, such as Alaska and Botswana, where cold and heat constrained intensive settlement, a higher proportion of land has been defined as parks at about 28 and 15 per cent respectively. Considerably more land in the United States and South Africa qualifies for less stringent protection as state and provincial parks, wildlife reserves/ refuges and forests. In the former, Wilderness Areas (both within and outside of parks) represent the most demanding category of federal land management. Parks are 'special' places but it should be remembered that a host of regulations govern human exploitation of vulnerable plant and animal species beyond their boundaries too.

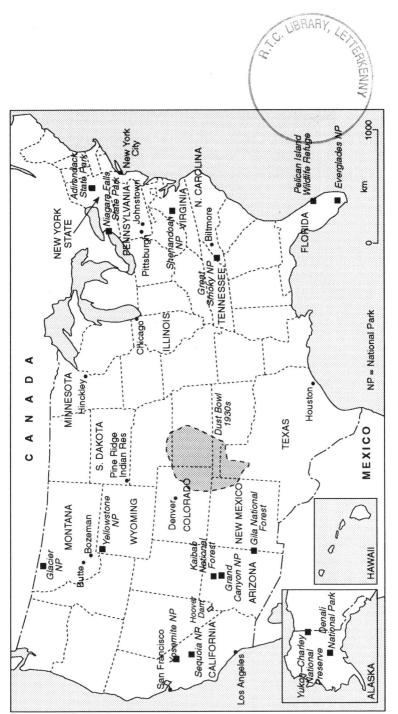

Map 3 Selected places and conservation units in the United States mentioned in the text

Map 4 Selected places and conservation units in South Africa mentioned in the text (1980s)

The development of areas for nature and its human clientele has a complex social history despite the apparent absence of a human presence: science, urban growth, aesthetic understandings, cultural nationalism, art, tourism, photography and film have all shaped ideas about nature. Though the pioneering American example has influenced South Africa (as it has the rest of the world) their park histories have flowed in distinctive channels. In the United States, expansion westward into the dramatic scenery of the Rockies – graphically recorded on enormous canvasses – fuelled the park lobby as the urban northeast sought to define its relationship with the unfolding continent. Spectacle counted and the desire to shield the public interest from private exploitation enshrined Yosemite (state park, 1864; national park, 1890), Yellowstone (1872), Niagara Falls (state reservation, 1885), Sequoia (1890), and the Grand Canyon (1908), among others.

The demise of plants, birds and animals (see chapter 2) certainly engendered concern but did not supply the crucial early momentum.

Rather it was the attempt to forge a national identity out of natural grandeur – all the more compelling because the United States found it difficult to compete with Europe in the high cultural stakes. Americans located their ancient and hallowed relics not in crown jewels and gothic cathedrals but in redwoods and 'purple mountain majesties'. (Resonances are found, if later, in the South African celebration of '*ewige gebergte waar die kranse aantwoord gee*' – the echoing ravines of everlasting mountains.) Despite the high cultural value which preservationists placed on parks, Congressional enactment was largely determined by the apparent absence of natural resource potential. Most parks, Yellowstone excepted, were restricted to the topographically spectacular.

In South Africa the primary impulse for reservation derived from late nineteenth-century concerns about predatory hunting and the disappearance of game species with which the region was so prolifically blessed. Game reserves, first discussed and enforced in the 1880s, were a response to the failure of hunting laws. In 1886, Cape regulations attempted to co-ordinate effective protection for big game, and in 1889 the Pongola reserve was demarcated just south of Swaziland. The idea took root in its most potent guise in the Sabi and Singwitsi reserves of the eastern Transvaal. Neither these nor the early Natal reserves were scenically distinctive. Most were bushveld areas, attractive for the variety of their woodland, birds and animals rather than for soaring peaks or rushing rivers.

James Stevenson-Hamilton, long-serving first warden of the Sabi reserve, had been a typical late Victorian soldier and hunter. But after the South African War, which witnessed destructive hunting by irregular soldiers in the eastern Transvaal, he rapidly came to appreciate the scientific case for preservation. Though initially reluctant to grant all animals equal stature – he shot out predators such as wild dogs which are now among the rarest African mammals – he helped swing bureaucratic opinion toward complete protection. The Report of the Game Reserves Commission in 1918 incorporated the idea that wildlife should be preserved in its entirety and not solely as isolated game species. Just as imperial hunting was once regarded as an outdoor academy for soldiers, the report's authors envisaged that reserves would serve as training ground for zoologists and botanists; animal behaviour could be studied in an area less affected by hunting 'which in other parts of the country tend[s] completely to alter their habits' (Carruthers, 1989: 205).

Though there were American proponents of wildlife preservation advancing ostensibly élitist arguments that parks should serve as field laboratories, US park policy was conditioned by a democratic tradition which prioritized public access. So the majority of rangers catered to entertainment-craving tourists giving rise to charming scenes of 'teddy bear picnics' (with honey, of course) and deer begging from cars. The National Park Service only pushed this scientific case up the agenda with its report on *Fauna of the National Parks of the United States* (1933). 'Awesome scenery', it cautioned, also needed 'the intimate details of living things, the plants, the animals that live on them' (Runte, 1979: 111). The Great Smoky Mountain (1934) and Shenandoah (1935) national parks, set in the much more subdued Appalachians in the east, were partly justified on the grounds of their botanical richness but were essentially reserved as picturesque mountain areas within reach of dense urban agglomerations. The one partial exception, and less secure for that reason, was the Everglades park in Florida (1934) – dismissed by traditionalists in the park movement as a featureless and pestilential swamp.

Powerful forces within settler society opposed large game reserves and parks. Farmers and ranchers, mining companies and land speculators all had an interest in encroaching on protected land or in restricting expansion. Entomologists and veterinarians concerned about the spread of the tsetse fly on the backs of its wildlife hosts opposed parks in northern Natal. Dr Ernest Warren, the moving force behind these game reserves, saw Sir David Bruce, one of the discoverers of the trypanosome, as the 'arch-enemy of the wild animals of Africa' (Brooks, 1990: 73). In 1920, the Umfolozi reserve was abolished in the face of an alliance between farmers and veterinarians. However, in the longer term, a compromise was achieved with reproclamation of the reserve under tighter management of wildlife. Cattle owners in the eastern Transvaal, emboldened by veterinary advances that widened their grazing range, badgered the government for access. But the Sabi and Singwitsi reserves survived, partly because of the fecundity of the mosquitoes and ticks they harboured.

Reserved areas in South Africa were at the mercy of deproclamation due to their shaky local legal foundations while even Congressionally mandated American parks could have their boundaries redrawn to exclude valuable natural resources. Hence the importance of cultivating a broad-based clientele and of establishing a formal system of park management with a strong institutional basis in the shape of the US National Park Service (1916) and the parliamentary legislation for the Kruger national park (1926).

Drawing on the American literature, Carruthers argues that the creation of Kruger depended less on public support for conservation than on the surge of white nationalism. (Early game reserves had been largely inaccessible to the general public – unlike many American parks, into which branch lines ran off the trunk western rail routes.) Kruger's name was explicitly invoked by the largely English-speaking propagandists of the national parks to lend the campaign legitimacy in the eyes of Afrikaners, recently victorious in a national election (1924). Pioneers of the past had gorged on game but the value of wildlife could be reinterpreted for a new generation who would be able to see the landscape 'just as the Voortrekkers saw it' (Reitz, quoted in Carruthers, 1989: 208). Intriguingly, game animals became a recurrent motif in white South Africa's conception and projection of itself. Assorted wildlife were emblazoned on postage stamps – the springbok's head became the watermark soon after Union in 1910 and first displaced the king's head in 1926, the year that the Kruger national park was founded. The springbok sold almost everything from cigarettes to the national airline; wildlife was the staple of tourist brochures. American publicists offered their parks in like style as places for vicarious pioneering in pristine landscapes redolent of the continent on the eve of white settlement. A thick cultural mantle clothed nature's naked contours.

The zoological preoccupations of South African nature conservationists, derived more strongly from imperial and local ideas than from American, continued to dominate park policy. Striking scenery was protected at Giant's Castle game reserve in the Natal Drakensberg (1903), but more typical motives were on display in the dense Addo bush of the eastern Cape where an isolated herd of small elephants survived. Protected from the late nineteenth century, the herd had grown sufficiently for local farmers to call for their extermination and in 1919 most were culled. The slaughter sparked a public reaction and Addo was entrenched as a national park in 1931. The provision of water sources in the park helped to keep the herd out of farms. The huge desert Kalahari Gemsbok national park was declared in 1930 to protect this rare species of oryx, as well as springbok and hartebeest. And the mountain zebra, almost following the quagga to extinction, was granted a small national refuge in the eastern Cape. A sea change appears to have taken place in South African attitudes towards wild animals at this time. It was symbolized by the extensive media coverage given to the marine adventures of Huberta, a female hippopotamus who swam over 1,000 km. down the east coast from northern Natal between 1928 and 1931. Huberta disregarded the boundaries of civilization and landed to browse in such places as the Durban Country Club golf course; in turn she captured the hearts of a budding wildlife constituency (Skead, 1987: 906). Outside the national parks, conservation remained a provincial responsibility and, as in the case of US state governments, provinces could create their own reserves. In the case of English-dominated Natal, the provincial parks board effectively took over game conservation after 1947. Through its campaign to save and then disperse the white rhino it became a national trend-setter.

Tourism had not been the primary argument for the first parks or reserves. But the pulling power of American natural wonders and South African wildlife was not lost on their early champions. Beauty and value were easily associated. The region's scenic 'grandeur', American geographer Henry Gannett exclaimed of Alaska in the *National Geographic Magazine* (1901), 'measured in direct returns in money received from tourists . . . is more valuable than the gold or the fish or the timber, for it will never be exhausted' (Nash, 1982: 283). Tourism, it was soon recognized, provided a pay-off for the investment in protected national areas. Stevenson-Hamilton studied the promotional methods of the boosterist American national park service closely. Piet Grobler, minister of lands at the time of South African park legislation and a relation of Kruger, was convinced by the success of American initiatives in this sphere. Land spared the hoof, the axe, the pick and the plough was none the less commoditized.

Just as they carried pioneers to newly opened farmlands, western US railroads were a conduit for eastern travellers seeking space and spectacle. 'See America First' campaigns explicitly competed with European-bound luxury liners, touting America's snow-capped mountain parks as rivals to the Swiss Alps. The tours of South African Railways were instrumental in winning the public over to the proposed Kruger national park. And like the Union Castle steamship line, the main passenger service from Britain, it increasingly capitalized on game in its advertising. Travellers on the 2,000-kilometre line from Cape Town to the Victoria Falls could reconcile themselves to the monotony of the veld with the promise of game viewing in Zimbabwe.

Automobiles soon changed the tempo of tourism, rendering the parks accessible to independent white middle-class travellers. In 1928 130,000 cars entered Yosemite and the national parks and monuments *in toto* attracted 3 million people the following year. The Kruger national park, which was visited by 180 cars in 1928, was pulling 30,000 visitors annually by the late 1930s. Given the comparative number of cars in South Africa and the United States, however, game viewing had evidently become almost as important a tourist experience for whites. Southern African tourism was beginning to resemble the American popular mode, rather than the élite imperial safari that clung on in East Africa. (Karen Blixen's lover in her autobiographical work, *Out of Africa*, Denys Finch-Hatton, made his living from this trade.)

A stark difference remained in that Americans could camp out in their national parks, even if they were not yet hitting the hiking trails. After a few years of armed camping in the wild, South Africans were obliged to remain in their rondavels and Fords in view of the risk from dangerous animals. The numerous lions, a major initial attraction, proved to be undisturbed by humans in cars, though they reacted more unpredictably to those on foot. After a party of American visitors contracted malaria, the Kruger park's perils were further minimized in 1930 by the closure of much of its area in the wet and sweaty summer months (Stevenson-Hamilton, 1952/1993: ch. 10). South African authorities thus found it easier to direct and contain the impact of visitors. In a country where public ownership of key resources was widely established, they could also control accommodation and services within their boundaries, whereas the tourist infrastructure in US parks was operated by a brash private sector that lost no opportunity to display its entrepreneurial fireworks. A long time would pass before South Africans would have to confront the tensions between the parks' dual mandate of trusteeship of natural heritage on the one hand and development in the interests of recreation on the other. By the 1970s, well over 40 million visited American national parks and monuments annually, whereas the South Africa figure was little over half a million.

First-hand experience of wild nature in this fashion (even if through the automobile windscreen) must be situated within a longer tradition of curiosity about a spectacular world that challenged European notions of civilization and control. Public interest in evolution and natural history reached the proportions of what John MacKenzie calls a 'craze' (1988: 37), not only in Britain where it was incorporated into the school curriculum in the late nineteenth century but also in Australia and across the Atlantic where it was complemented by a classroom nature study movement. Part of this phenomenon was the massive popularity of tales of hunting and natural history writings. By the early twentieth century, the success of these narratives was assured by books such as Jack London's *The Call of the Wild* (1903) and Edgar Rice Burroughs's *Tarzan of the Apes* (1914). In Britain, the enduring appeal of adventure sagas such as *King Solomon's Mines* moulded youthful perceptions of foreign parts. Baden-Powell's Boy Scouts (1907), bristling with hunting and tracking lore, flourished on both sides of the Atlantic. The movement was anticipated and directly influenced by the American naturalist Ernest Thompson Seton's Woodcraft Indians and Daniel Carter Beard's Sons of Daniel Boone. In the 1920s, a less militaristic British Woodcraft movement (later the Woodcraft Folk) was launched which incorporated girls as well as boys (Wheen, 1991).

Like the model of muscular Christianity and the Etonian playing fields, the Rooseveltian celebration of the strenuous life promoted an association between personal virility and national prowess. Images of the gun-toting Boer commando at the turn of the century provided a surprising role model to contrast with the physical puniness of stunted British volunteers in the South African war – misshapen products of vice-filled city life (Brogan, 1987: 27). These associations were nurtured by the strength of environmental determinism in both intellectual and popular language at the turn of the century.

Evocative lithographs of wildlife encounters were a mandatory accompaniment to nineteenth-century adventure stories. The increasing availability of quality visual representation in the form of photographs and stereoscopic slides sharpened the focus of these images. Pioneer photographer William Henry Jackson distributed his photographs of Yellowstone in handsome portofolios to Congressmen in a bid to win them over to the cause of the national park. Professional wildlife photographers such as Arthur Dugmore, author of *Nature and the Camera* (1902), supplied the needs of nature book publishers at the beginning of the century. New printing methods delivered the glossy photographs that heralded the coffee table nature book and were deployed to great advantage by railroad companies advertising their scenic routes. This powerful medium became a household institution in the pages of the mass circulation *National Geographic Magazine*.

The first moving picture images of the US national parks (Glacier, 1903; Yellowstone, 1909) were filmed at the same time, and the vanguard role of Americans in the industry gave American audiences direct access to African animals. Film-making initially replicated the literary hunting saga, placing a premium on action, challenge, death and charismatic protagonists, both human and animal. As early as 1912, *African Hunt*, made by Paul J. Rainey, a wealthy American big game hunter, grossed $500,000. Martin Johnson accompanied Jack London to the South Seas and then made a living showing lantern slides in small-town America. He translated his vaudeville experience into feature films on Africa which included manufactured events in which rhinos, elephants and lions were induced to charge at the camera.

In the 1920s Carl Akeley, a leading figure at the American Museum of Natural History, an expert on the gorilla and the African elephant, persuaded Johnson and his wife to follow a less sensationalist path. Fearing that the fate of the American bison awaited many large African mammals, Akeley got his museum into the educational movie business by raising money for long filming sessions to record African game for posterity. As part of this venture, Akeley devoted considerable time to producing a more versatile and durable movie camera. George Eastman, recognizing the potential of the genre for the industry, visited both him and the Johnsons in Kenya (Bodry-Sanders, 1991: 142–4, 208–13). A series of African films released in the late 1920s and early 1930s which interspersed 'thrills and spills' with careful conservationist observation were a major economic success, attracting audiences of hundreds of thousands. Southern and eastern African themes also enjoyed a high profile in American sports hunting periodicals at this time.

Despite the new urban-industrial, cosmopolitan mentality associated with the Jazz Age, 1920s America witnessed a spate of outdoor movies. Thundering waterfalls were an even bigger selling point than turbulent sex in the roaring twenties. Until the 1930s, a highly exploitative approach dominated animal film-making. Frank Buck's *Bring 'Em Back Alive* (1932) featured a staged fight to the death between an orang-utan and a tiger, despite the objections of his cameraman and his animal handler who protested that these animals would never meet in the wild (Denis, 1963). This approach to the wild was epitomized by the smash hit feature film, *King Kong* (1933). A more careful approach, however, building on the Johnsons' finest footage and unobtrusive techniques (long hours crouched in hides), began to establish itself after the Second World War. Armand Denis's *Savage Splendour*, which confirmed this commitment to educational and conservation film, was RKO's most profitable feature film of 1949 and set the scene for the famous Disney 'True Life Adventure' series that included *The Living Desert* (1953). When nature film made the transition to television in the early 1950s, spearheaded in Britain by Denis and the former South African hunter, George Michael, it became the most influential new medium for envisioning the wild in the metropolitan world.

Trends in wildlife film popularized new scientific approaches that internationalized conservation thinking in a way which could incorporate American predilections for extravagant scenery as well as the wildlife-oriented South Africans. A major element in these approaches from the 1920s was the rise of ecology as the study of interconnections between animals, plants and their physical locale. The word habitat, an eighteenth-century natural history term originally used mainly by botanists, was entering common parlance. Zoology as a discipline increasingly emphasized the study of animals in their natural environs. Late nineteenth-century specimen collecting for the great natural history museums of London and New York, as well as the colonial collections in Cape Town and Pretoria, expressed a natural history preoccupied with classifying animals, examining them dead and recording their proportions. Live animal behaviour tended to be explored in the proliferating zoological gardens. From the 1940s, less emphasis was placed on attempts to bring large apes back alive *à la* King Kong; instead, naturalists dedicated much of their lives to observing 'the year of the gorilla' on inhospitable mountain slopes in central Africa.

BIOCENTRISM AND PARK POLITICS

Ecological concepts were just beginning to find their niche within conservation. US historians have offered Aldo Leopold and his ideas as the crucial link between turn-of-the century natural resource conservation and a modern environmentalism informed by a recognition of the complexity and interdependence of all parts of the natural world. Leopold cut his teeth in the US forest service where he imbibed Pinchot's utilitarian notions until he quit in the late 1920s to explore a more holistic vision. Leopold's conversion experience was triggered by his participation in successful predator cleansing campaigns in the 1920s, which led to the rapid expansion of deer which then overgrazed their range within the Kaibab National Forest to the north of the Grand Canyon. The deer population soon crashed, which Leopold interpreted as a supreme object lesson in 'the value of a varmint'. This incident, which has attained the status of gospel through incantation based on his influential posthumous *A Sand County Almanac* (1949), opened the doors of his perception:

> I now suspect that just as a deer herd lives in mortal fear of its wolves, so does a mountain live in mortal fear of its deer. And perhaps with better cause, for while a buck pulled down by wolves can be replaced in two or three years, a range pulled down by too many deer may fail of replacement in as many decades.
>
> (Leopold, 1949: 132)

The recent reinterpretation of the Kaibab sequence by wildlife biologists, who suggest that predator control as a factor in rising deer levels has been exaggerated, does not undermine the potency of his parable.[1]

Leopold's insights into the malfunctioning that could result from human interventions was extended in the classic studies by the Murie brothers in the 1930s on wolves and coyotes for the National Park Service, which was routinely destroying predators at the time. These studies suggested unappreciated benefits accruing from stable predator populations in maintaining the health of the land. The lives of sheep and a few calves might be lost but the proliferation of locusts, rabbits, mice and other rodents, all of which consumed vegetation, would be checked.

In the South African context at roughly the same time, zoologists had acknowledged the value of scavengers such as jackals as 'nature's sanitary corps' (Fitzsimons, 1919: 92ff.). Stevenson-Hamilton declared in 1926: 'I think that the ideal should be to show the country and the animals in it to the public as God made both', which meant the inclusion of lions, subsequently the most popular animal in the Kruger park (Carruthers, 1989: 215). Opposition to the use of poison was already finding focus in dismay over the loss of snake-eating secretary birds which succumbed to the bait intended for vermin. In 1933, the London meeting of the Convention for the Protection of African Flora and Fauna attacked the very concept of vermin (aside from rats and the like). Aficionados of the eagle were by the 1940s convinced that the costs of its loss as a dassie eater far outweighed the benefits that farmers might have gained through saving a few lambs. A dassie is now estimated to consume a seventh the amount of pasture as a sheep. Sportsmen seized on the new findings, arguing rather spuriously that hunters filled a crucial niche often left vacant by predator eradication. At least among naturalists, this changing set of concerns manifested itself in new management strategies within parks.

In addition to catering for a swelling tourist population, park professionals also aimed for a better 'balance' of species. The small and ordinary as well as the large and extraordinary, inconspicuous bushes as well as towering trees, the sharp-fanged as well as the doe-eyed were valued as citizens of equal standing in the ecological community. It was also necessary, however, to restrict the number of animals to the food and water resources available (the notion of carrying capacity). In some instances, this involved a reversal of policy. Growing benevolence toward the once-maligned was accompanied by culling by slaughter or sale of grazers and browsers.

The stress on ecology, so fundamental to park professionals, was not easily transmitted to a broader public. More readily broadcast through the new medium of television was the potential of an attractive intimacy with savage animals. TV brought such endearing images of interaction into the living rooms of Europe and the United States more effectively than photos or film.[2] Powerful protagonists of these relationships, some of whom were innovative film-makers, consciously projected these values. Armand and Michaela Denis, who set up shop in Nairobi to make television films for the BBC in 1953, kept a menagerie of animals in their backyard, including Voodoo the vulture. George Michael, whose features on the BBC preceded the Denises', filled his Pretoria garden with (segregated) pet lions and springbok. George and Joy Adamson hit the headlines in the early 1960s when they publicized their adventure with Elsa, a motherless lioness cub they had adopted in 1956.

> How little did Joy or I imagine that the story of the smallest of the three cubs . . . would be translated into thirty-three languages, sell several million copies, be made into a film and, as we hope and believe, made a lasting impact on the way in which human beings regard the wild animals.
>
> (Adamson, 1968: 219)

Armand Denis also claims to have made one of the first television films highlighting elephant poaching in Kenya. (In fact, the Kruger national park was producing such films in the 1940s.) So convinced were these conservationists of the righteousness of their cause that they, reflecting broader colonial preoccupations, overlooked claims that indigenous peoples might have on reserved land. Protection of elephants and buffalo in South African state forests in the nineteenth century had entailed forced removal of African villages to often waterless sites without any compensation. Game conservation, even when it became ecologically and habitat oriented, was an increasingly exclusive pursuit where the only legitimate human roles were those of ranger, scientist and camera-clicking tourist.

A prolonged war of attrition had been fought out along the eastern boundary of the Kruger park where some of the 'poachers' had previously had access to the land for hunting. While new police posts along the border with Mozambique in the 1930s helped contain the problem, park boundaries were never entirely secure (Trapido, 1984). Much of what was defined as poaching in and around the Natal parks, situated in the midst of dense African settlement in Zululand, represented a continuation of day-by-day hunting activity by African communities. People took small antelope to supplement dwindling meat supplies and sold the skins. 'Whenever the native happens to be in want of some money, all he does is to go and sell a few game skins to the sugar planters, in the form of riems, straps, whips . . .', lamented a park warden (Brooks, 1990: 50).

Poaching assumed many guises, from motorized European trophy hunting to Africans seeking subsistence. Many Africans would not recognize the new spatial boundaries. The position was further complicated by policies that permitted intensive game sweeps to clear private farmland of tsetse hosts while all wildlife within contiguous but often unfenced game parks was strictly out of bounds. In Natal, where smaller parks, white-owned farmland and African reserves abutted one another, the dilemma was particularly acute. Even in the period after the Second World War, hand-to-hand battles and gunfights between poachers and rangers were commonplace. The best-known African ranger and oral historian of wildlife, Magqubu Ntombela, graphically described one such encounter, where he shot an aggressive poacher caught quartering a warthog (Steele, 1968: 63).

Conflict with communities who believed park resources to be their own was a lesser feature of the American scene outside Alaska, since park was fashioned out of public lands that had already been effectively depopulated. The Euro-American perception of wilderness, to paraphrase one commentator hostile to its preservation, is that of a physical environment freeze-framed at the point after the Indians have been cleared away but before the settlers have arrived. In the early 1850s, US troops flushed the final Ahwahneechee Indians out of one of the last strongholds of resistance in California to white invasion during the gold rush – Yosemite Valley. The park-like landscape of meadows dotted with spreading black oak so pleasing to nineteenth-century white aesthetic canons was the product of Indian firing. Within a few years, the first tourists had arrived and those Indians who had not retreated to a reservation found work in the valley's hotels, the most opulent of which bore the name of their tribe. A Miwok village survived down to the 1960s, though it is never mentioned in the rapturous paeans to an unblemished wilderness paradise.

In Alaska, by contrast, Native peoples still comprise the majority population over the greater part of what is by far the largest American state. Though amounting to only 16 per cent of the state's population, they live predominantly in small villages widely dispersed in the 'bush'. The discovery of oil at Prudhoe Bay in 1968 precipitated the dividing up of Alaska's unappropriated public lands, a process that included the formal granting in 1971 of outright ownership of 10 per cent of the state to its Native peoples – but in return for the extinguishing of aboriginal claims to the entire state. Massive additions to the national park system (1980) – which more than doubled its size at a stroke – were the highlight of the conservationists' slice of the Alaskan pie (Coates, 1993). As these units were imposed in areas with long traditions of Native natural resource use, they accommodated Native subsistence hunting, gathering and trapping. Also permissible as 'traditional' since the 1960s were forms of mechanized access by snow machine, outboard motor, all-terrain vehicle and bush plane – activities and technologies proscribed in previous US parks and frowned on by wilderness purists. For the more uncompromising environmentalist, hunting with a harpoon from a skin kayak wearing sealskin boots is correct subsistence; pursuit with a high calibre rifle on a snowmobile wearing rubber boots is a sham. In further recognition of the special circumstances of Alaska, a new category of federal protection was created, the national preserve, in which sports hunting and commercial trapping are permitted. Alaskan parks are less developed than other American parks in that the majority have no roads, hotels, campgrounds or other visitor facilities. At the same time, airplane access and all-terrain vehicles have annihilated the remoteness of parks hundreds of miles away from even an unpaved road (Coates, 1990).

Within their terms of reference, South African parks were a signal success. The power of the state facilitated comprehensive controls over the boundaries of nature reserves. Whereas there were barely a couple of hundred elephants at the turn of the century in the country as a whole, over 8,000 roamed the land by the 1980s. In neighbouring Namibia, Botswana and Zimbabwe, the rise was even more spectacular. While underfinanced parks in much of the rest of Africa have experienced severe losses of elephants – so that continent-wide figures have fallen from over a million to 600,000 – elephant numbers in Botswana, South Africa, Zimbabwe and Namibia have boomed (Barbier *et al.*, 1990: 67). The nature of poaching changed by the 1970s when the bulk of losses were no longer from wire traps but from gangs with firearms and direct links with middlemen involved in the Far Eastern ivory trade. Civil warfare, especially in Mozambique and Angola, decimated game stocks even more rapidly than commercial poaching. Not only did troops live off the land but Renamo and Unita peddled ivory for arms. Rising prices through to the 1980s sustained the tusk trade. Poachers tend to go for large males with big tusks, leaving a preponderance of younger males and females with long-term implications for breeding.

From the 1950s, South African conservation policy began to take on board the idea of habitat rather than species preservation. The new parks developed from the 1970s especially, such as the Karoo national park, had no eye-catching animals and, indeed, had to be repopulated with selected species. The municipality of Beaufort West was persuaded to relinquish a large area of commonage, which was extended to include 'typical' Karoo mountain and plains habitats. Coastal reserves, both national and provincial, were chosen for their representative flora and birds rather than their distinctive mammals.

American park advisers were thinking along the same lines in the 1960s and 1970s. A. Starker Leopold, following in his father's footsteps, chaired a special park service wildlife advisory board whose report reiterated the 'enormous complexity of ecological communities' – echoing recommendations from the 1933 report concerning 'the preservation of characteristic portions of our country' (Runte, 1979: 153; 1990: 179). Scientists had in a sense caught up with George Catlin, the nineteenth-century artist and ethnographer, and Walt Whitman, the arch-spokesman of cultural nationalism, in their recognition of the beauty and value of ordinary landscapes such as the topographically featureless grasslands.

This latest conservationist thrust has been less successful in the USA than in South Africa – a testament to the limits of federal power and the obduracy of farmers. The white South African Nationalist government was no less conservative politically and economically than America's presidency during the long Republican ascendancy (1980–92), but had the control and the conviction to pursue the statist conservationism that had historically characterized the country. The populist ethos and the local political primacy of private farmlands have to date frustrated attempts to create a Tallgrass Prairie National Preserve in Oklahoma.

Despite the constraints on national initiatives, a multiplicity of more local authorities could create other categories of reserved land. The Adirondack state park in upstate New York – the biggest US park outside Alaska – contains both forested mountains (small by trans-Mississippian standards) and rolling countryside. Unlike provincial nature reserves in South Africa, however, extensive use and occupation, including private property and village settlements, continued. Up to a 100,000 people live and work in the park and public access is limited by a profusion of 'no trespassing' signs on the 50 per cent of park lands that remain privately owned. This strategy has much in common with the concept of conservation which ruled in England and Wales, where a permanent and long-standing human presence also had to be incorporated. Legislation setting up national parks (1949) restricted private activity through planning controls rather than by actually taking the land into public ownership. State conservation in Britain argues that careful husbandry by farmers themselves sustains nature more efficiently and knowledgeably than any outside governmental authority. In a way, this reflects the difference between European perceptions of nature as an eminently cultural product and South African and American cultural hankerings after pristine wilderness or 'untouched' frontier landscapes.

Protecting wildlife and its habitats within reserves of any category or status, by its nature, must be a limited strategy, affecting relatively small areas of land and conforming to political and economic exigencies. Conservationists and commercial farmers have recently discovered shared interests in schemes involving non-reserved land. Private game reserves, a rapidly expanding feature of the South African countryside, are one striking example. Wealthy farmers and big corporate landowners have long kept a limited number of game animals for viewing and hunting. Indeed, a few species, such as the mountain zebra and bontebok, probably survived the critical early decades of the century through the efforts of individual farmers. Areas bordering on the Kruger national park, such as Timbavati, became major private game reserves open to visitors as well. Private parks have multiplied, especially in the Transvaal, as the economics of restocking farmland with indigenous game animals has become more favourable. Tourism, hunting and leisure sustain game farms; the most sophisticated boast hotels, camps, swimming pools and conference centres.

Surplus animals from state parks are sold on the private market and bused around the country to reintegrate nature into private lands. Game farms hold regular public auctions of wild animals, their price buoyed up by steady demand for breeding stock, venison and game biltong. The Willem Pretorius game reserve in the Orange Free State advertises 'Buffalo 10; Springbuck 360; Blesbuck 175; Gnu 265; Eland 20. . . . Lion 3', as well as twenty-four hunts in the 1994–95 season (*Farmer's Weekly*, 15 April 1994, 6). Secure control by private landowners of their game has been advocated by some free market enthusiasts as the surest way of preserving wildlife and their habitats in southern Africa where market forces, poverty and the loss of colonial certitude might place all state lands under intolerable pressure.

Operation Campfire, initiated by the Zimbabwean government in the 1980s, took policy a step further by attempting to introduce wildlife into African communal areas. Especially in dryer and more marginal farming zones, it was contended, wild animals were best adapted to exploiting local vegetation. The problem was to persuade locals to consume game rather than cattle, as well as recognize the ecological benefits. Proponents of popular environmentalism in South Africa, critical of the exclusivity of park policy, have succeeded in launching schemes where rural communities retain some rights to park resources (see chapter 6). One important example has been the recently declared Richtersveld national park in the northern Cape on the border with Namibia (1992), a fragile mountainous desert area with a unique botanical profile including rare succulents such as the *halfmensboom* (a tree half like a person.) 'When the community first heard that some of its pastoralists could be deported in the interests of conservation, one man commented: "Hulle gee om vir die halfmens, maar wat van die volmens?" ("They care about the half person, but what about the whole person?")' (Cock and Koch, 1991: 119).

Community spokespeople together with land activists persuaded the Parks Board that the local Nama people had grazed their stock in the area for centuries without irrevocably destroying it. After protracted negotiations, community access for grazing and the garnering of natural products such as honey was secured. A portion of park income was promised to a trust fund, guides would be recruited locally and opportunities developed for craft sales. These strategies have been conceived as a means of safeguarding the park by creating a local stake in it. Experiments of this kind, reflecting resolutions of the International Union for the Conservation of Nature in 1990, promise *détente* between parks and people – 'conservation with a human face' (Anderson and Grove, 1987: 79).

In Alaska, America's so-called 'last great wilderness frontier', proposals for new parks have aggrieved settlers as well as indigenous peoples. Sport hunting, firewood gathering and gold mining by often urban-based white Alaskans were curtailed in the new parks, whose regulations favoured subsistence uses by the 'rural resident' (mainly Native) who consumes fish and game. Perhaps most upset by the new restrictions were the predominantly white hunting guides, for trophy hunting is big business in Alaska – a favourite destination for the international sporting élite. The arrival of the first park personnel was often greeted with defiance. In one village that found a park as its new neighbour, a park service airplane was set alight and a ranger recalls how 'First day I arrived, a service station attendant refused to sell me gas.' Restaurants put up signs indicating that park service people would not be served (*National Geographic*, May 1994: 93).

But the disaffected group that has attracted most attention is the neo-pioneers who settled along the Yukon and its tributaries in east-central Alaska in the early 1970s. For these educated young refugees from modern America, the Yukon basin was the last place in the United States to reconnect with the venerable settler tradition of building a cabin in the woods and hunting, fishing and trapping for a living. Fortunately for these 'river people', the region dotted with their cabins, fish camps and trap lines became a preserve dedicated to the protection of cultural resources – where they can continue their lives, at least for the moment – rather than a park, from which they would have been evicted (McPhee, 1977).

In both Alaska and southern Africa, the new emphasis on partici-patory development and concession to human use has exciting and pioneering potential. This should not blind us to the pitfalls. On the one hand, modern humanity finds it very difficult not to carry the airplane, the auto and the rest of its bulging urban cultural baggage into the parks. On the other, impoverished and land-hungry Africans might find the temptations of the park resources irresistible once they get a foothold.

It may be hard to avoid more thorough resource exploitation and prevent the re-invention of highly commercial forms of reserve comparable to the pleasuring grounds of early twentieth-century Yosemite with its firefalls, tossing of live chickens into chasms, and rodeo. The former Bophuthatswana homeland government planned its Pilanesberg reserve as an adjunct to the huge holiday and gambling complex of Sun City.

The peopling of parks, by automobile-powered tourists and those seeking nature's solitude, poses management problems on a par with those presented by the flora and fauna. Income from wildlife watchers protects wild animals, so that a live elephant, metaphorically speaking, is worth its weight in ivory. But the price is the collapsing of the boundaries between consumer society and the wildness it seeks to create. In the most extreme instances, animal breeding and plant regeneration are disturbed by the growl of the microbus and pounding of boots along multi-lane trails.

Yet the larger societal significance of parks and reserves cannot be judged simply in terms of their capacity to enhance nature's patrimony. As in their formation a century or more ago, today's parks remain a powerful cultural statement fusing notions of nature and nation. Park policy-makers appreciate this. After hiking entry and accommodation prices to lure a better-heeled clientele, South African conservationists and wildlife lobbies are recognizing the importance of including blacks in their enterprise by providing lower-cost access. Nelson Mandela has participated in environmental films. In the USA, increasing visits by members of immigrant groups such as Asians is an intriguing badge of assimilation into a specifically national culture. Standing at the foot of Yosemite Falls constitutes, in a sense, an outdoor civics lesson. The Sierra Club runs a programme to introduce inner city youth, many of them black, to the charms and challenges of the wilderness. The future of parks and reserves in a rapidly changing political context might depend on the universalization both of a set of environmental values and of a non-racial sense of nature's heritage.

NOTES

1 Increased availability of browse due to livestock reduction and a deer-hunting ban may have been the operative factors.
2 Some commentators stress that the final estrangement of people from wild beast is taking place, with the latter relegated to children's books, zoo cages and safari parks. Yet through the burgeoning media of the natural history film on television, we are arguably more familiar with the intimate details of wildlife than at any time since our hunter-gatherer ancestors.

REFERENCES AND FURTHER READING

Abbey, Edward (1968) *Desert Solitaire*, New York: Random House.

Adams, Jonathan and McShane, Thomas O. (1992) *The Myth of Wild Africa: Conservation without Illusions*, New York: W.W. Norton.

Adamson, George (1968) *Bwana Game: The Life Story of George Adamson*, London: Collins Harvill.

Anderson, David and Grove, Richard (eds) (1987) *Conservation in Africa: People, Policies and Practice*, Cambridge: Cambridge University Press.

Barbier, Edward B., Burgess, Joanne C., Swanson, Timothy M. and Pearce, David W. (1990) *Elephants, Economics and Ivory*, London: Earthscan.

Bartlett, Richard A. (1985) *Yellowstone: A Wilderness Besieged*, Tucson: University of Arizona Press.

Bell, Ian (1987) 'Conservation with a human face: conflict and reconciliation in African land use planning', in David Anderson and Richard Grove (eds) (1987) *Conservation in Africa: People, Policies and Practice*, Cambridge: Cambridge University Press.

Bodry-Sanders, Penelope (1991) *Carl Akeley: Africa's Collector, Africa's Saviour*, New York: Paragon House.

Brogan, Hugh (1987) *Mowgli's Sons: Kipling and Baden-Powell's Scouts*, London: Cape.

Brooks, Shirley (1990) 'Playing the game: the struggle for wildlife protection in Zululand, 1910–1930', unpublished MA thesis, Queen's University, Kingston, Ontario, Canada.

Carruthers, Jane (1989) 'Creating a national park, 1910 to 1926', *Journal of Southern African Studies*, 15 (2), 188–216.

Chase, Alston (1986) *Playing God in Yellowstone: The Destruction of America's First National Park*, Boston: Atlantic Monthly Press.

Coates, Peter (1990) 'Re-enacting American history: white and Native American hunting ideologies in twentieth-century Alaska', unpublished paper, *Past and Present* conference on 'The Politics of Hunting', London.

—— (1993) *The Trans-Alaska Pipeline Controversy: Technology, Conservation and the Frontier*, Fairbanks: University of Alaska Press.

Cock, Jacklyn and Koch, Eddie (eds) (1991) *Going Green: People, Politics and the Environment in South Africa*, Cape Town: Oxford University Press.

Denis, Armand (1963) *On Safari*, London: Collins.

Dunlap, Thomas R. (1988) *Saving America's Wildlife: Ecology and the American Mind, 1850–1990*, Princeton, Princeton University Press.

Fitzsimons, F.W. (1919) *The Natural History of South African Mammals*, 4 vols; vol. 2, London: Longman, Green & Co.

Flader, Susan (1974) *Thinking Like a Mountain: Aldo Leopold and the Evolution of an Ecological Attitude Toward Deer, Wolves and Forests*, Columbia: University of Missouri Press.

Imperato, Pascal J. and Imperato, Eleanor M. (1992) *They Married Adventure: The Wandering Lives of Martin and Osa Johnson*, New Brunswick: Rutgers University Press.

Ise, John (1961) *Our National Parks: A Critical History*, Baltimore: Johns Hopkins University Press.

Leopold, Aldo (1949) *A Sand County Almanac*, New York: Oxford University Press.

MacKenzie, John (1988) *The Empire of Nature*, Manchester: Manchester University Press.

McPhee, John (1977) *Coming into the Country*, New York: Farrar, Straus.

Marnham, Patrick (1987) *Fantastic Invasion: Dispatches from Africa*, London: Penguin.

Mighetto, Lisa (1991) *Wild Animals and American Environmental Ethics*, Tucson: University of Arizona Press.

Murie, Adolf (1944) *The Wolves of Mount McKinley*, Washington, D.C.: National Park Service, Department of the Interior.

Nash, Roderick (1982) *Wilderness and the American Mind*, New Haven: Yale University Press.

Rothman, Hal (1989) *Preserving Different Pasts: The American National Monuments*, Champaign: University of Illinois Press.

Runte, Alfred (1979) *National Parks: The American Experience*, Lincoln: University of Nebraska Press.

—— (1990) *Yosemite: The Embattled Wilderness*, Lincoln: University of Nebraska Press.

Sax, Joseph L. (1980) *Mountains Without Handrails: Reflections on the National Parks*, Ann Arbor: The University of Michigan Press.

Skead, C.J. (1987) *Historical Mammal Incidence in the Cape Province*, vol. 2, *The Eastern Half of the Cape Province*, Cape Town: Provincial Administration of the Cape of Good Hope.

Steele, Nick (1968) *Game Ranger on Horseback*, Cape Town: Books of Africa.

Stevenson-Hamilton, James (1952, 1993) *South African Eden*, Cape Town: Struik.

Trapido, Stanley (1984) 'Poachers, proletarians and gentry in the early twentieth-century Transvaal', unpublished paper given at the African Studies Institute, University of the Witwatersrand.

Wheen, Francis (1991) 'The Green Shirts', *The Independent Magazine*, 5 October, 34–40.

Worster, Donald (1977) *Nature's Economy: A History of Ecological Ideas*, San Francisco: Sierra Club Books.

6   From conservation to environmentalism and beyond

National parks and wildlife protection have proved attractive magnets for white environmental concern because they furnish a route out of the central conservationist dilemma: how to enjoy the advantages of urban-industrial society while salvaging a modicum of nature. Protected areas, as we have illustrated, though 'special' places, are by no means unaffected by the smog of the very civilization apparently kept at arm's length. Air pollution from coal-fired power stations can reduce visibility at the Grand Canyon to a distance less than is required to see from one rim across to the other. Fears are growing that if a major mining venture goes ahead in the surrounding watershed, the integrity of Yellowstone national park's rivers will be threatened. Accordingly, the more challenging problem for conservationists of all kinds remains hard decisions about daily relationships with nature across the entire spectrum of environments, more or less natural, from the ordinary to the extraordinary. This implies an adaption of environmental concerns to the key areas of production and consumption in our urban and agricultural heartlands.

ENVIRONMENTAL IDEAS

In this chapter, we will first explore the dominant narrative of western environmentalism and then attempt to complement its thrust with an analysis of third world preoccupations and the environmentalism of the poor. American historians have been entranced by the search for environmentalism's intellectual and historical roots (Oelschlaeger, 1991). Though such debates over humankind's appropriate place in nature enjoy a lengthy pedigree (Glacken, 1967), a particular strain has been isolated which seemed to pose the most basic questions. The starting point is often taken to be early nineteenth-century romanticism and primitivism, initially associated with Wordsworth and Rousseau, that connected individual creativity, happiness and fulfilment with proximity to unmodified nature. Nature in its wilder forms served as a stick with which to beat the idea of progress and the worship of economic growth. Green academia has fixed on the anti-materialist scepticism of New England transcendentalists Ralph Waldo Emerson and Henry David Thoreau, delighting in the former's lament that 'Things are in the saddle and ride mankind' (Nash, 1982: 86–7).

John Muir, founder of the Sierra Club (1892), took up the torch at the turn of the century and operated in an increasingly sympathetic climate of opinion shaped by the perceived closing of the frontier and the appearance of old world urban-industrial scourges. Aldo Leopold and his biocentric philosophy (see chapter 5), conventionally identified as the next link in the chain with the present, was rediscovered in the 1960s when environmentalism became a popular middle-class ideology for the first time.

The mood of the 1950s and 1960s produced a set of preoccupations that had ramifications far beyond the more particular anxieties of conservation's founding fathers. In the US and other developed northern nations, a grassroots[1] 'protest' movement had emerged, uncomfortable with the rampant modernism, social conservatism and naïve technophilia of the post-war economic boom. Environmentalism matured alongside other questioning initiatives such as anti-consumerism, anti-war, feminism and civil rights that flourished in the reformist climate of the 1960s and 1970s. Each had its own distinctive history but they coalesced and were mutually enhancing as part of a youthful countercultural critique of dominant values and structures (half the US population was under 25 in 1970). The leitmotif of the new conservation was not so much the protection of particular components of the environment such as trees, soil or wildlife, but a broad-ranging confrontation with the insidious by-products of industrialism. Production methods developed since 1945 accounted for some 80 per cent of all pollutants by 1970. Environmentalism was conditioned by the new post-war order of big science and technology, their marriage to big business and the spread of affluence and effluence.

Anti-pollution drives in the US and Britain reach back to the nineteenth century and took definite shape in the turn-of-the-century Progressive reform era through civic improvement campaigns, often led by women, such as those of Alice Hamilton in Chicago against industrial poisons like lead and phosphorus (Gottlieb, 1993 a and b). The notorious London smog of 1952 (Brimblecombe, 1987: 161–78) and those of Pittsburgh in the 1940s were highly visual manifestations – like the dust storms of the 1930s – of the human tendency to foul its own nest. Whereas smog, dust and clear-cut forest provided immediate and striking evidence of environmental damage, many of the gravest environmental threats were becoming invisible and incremental in their impact. Nineteenth-century conservationists faced problems that were mild in comparison. Most had assumed that sky and water were inviolate, and menaces to human life itself did not enter the picture.

Pesticides, after their glowing military record in the Second World War against the likes of typhus-bearing lice, were redeployed on the home front in an offensive against the enemies of the suburban garden and golf course: the insects and weeds that threatened the latest version of the pastoral dream. The lawn was a new form of monoculture, just as vulnerable to insects and weeds and requiring almost as much fuel, water and fertilizer per acre as the average cornfield. The new poisons were just as warmly embraced by farmers as a miracle cure, 'nuking' pests which had long bugged them. In southern Africa, DDT's potential against tsetse fly and the mosquitoes which carried malaria was enormous. Major campaigns were launched in areas on the northern rim of the country and Natal, still susceptible to tropical diseases. Large parts of Zimbabwe were also drenched with DDT in the 1950s in a bid to eradicate the tsetse. The American South too was doused, in a vainglorious effort to expunge the boll weevil once and for all.

Rachel Carson's *Silent Spring* (1962), the improbable bestseller, made the arcane agricultural term, pesticides, a household word and a searing public issue. The book was instantly dubbed 'the *Uncle Tom's Cabin* of the environmental movement'.[2] A major factor in its success was the way in which Carson, a marine biologist and accomplished popular science writer, linked traditional wildlife protection issues with urban-industrial ones. The title evoked the deathlike silence of a small-town spring once heralded by a chorus of birdsong. Though not an avowed feminist, Carson injected a gender dimension into the environmental debate; modern science came across as a hard male onslaught with imperialistic designs on a softer feminine nature.

The enthusiastic reception of *Silent Spring* (serialized in *The New Yorker*) can be explained in part by the decade-long discussion of the harmful effects of nuclear fallout. In the wake of the Manhattan Project, both western and eastern parts of the developed world were mesmerized by the power and potential of the atom. Atomic power was seized upon as a solution to energy problems as well as a route to global dominance. The visual beauty of the mushroom cloud, captured on film and television, obscured its hidden menace. Identification of the longevity of damaging radiation was a telling lesson in the interrelatedness of all forms of planetary life within a single system, which predisposed the public to Carson's message about the accumulation of poisons within the food chain (Lutts, 1985; Coates, 1989a).

Barry Commoner, another trained biologist, traced isotopes from surface tests in Nevada in the 1950s via grass and cow's milk into human baby teeth where they resurfaced as high concentrations of radioactive strontium-90. In the later 1960s, the most resonant metaphor for the ubiquity of industrial impacts and vulnerability of even the remotest parts of the globe was the DDT found in the fatty tissues of Antarctic penguins. The anti-nuclear movement was fuelled by a burning moral concern about the destructive capacity of these unprecedented weapons as well as growing knowledge about their detrimental impact on the health of all species. Just as war was too serious to be left to generals, so science could not safely be left to ambitious chemists and physicists (rather than biologists) blinkered by the demands of the so-called military-industrial complex.

Those who acted to conserve supplies of trees, soil and water in the late nineteenth and earlier twentieth century, despite their fraught rhetoric, were convinced that human ingenuity in the shape of science and technology could coax ever more out of nature's store. Much of modern western environmentalism, by contrast, questions the very techniques and products of science applied to industrial production. Activists were galvanized by disaster scenarios revolving around industrial pollution such as nuclear meltdowns, lakes dying from detergent, sewage and chemical fertilizer overload, inflammable rivers, oil tanker spills, drilling platform blowouts and acid rain. No longer was the propelling motive a concern with the conservation of depleting natural resources but with the spoiling of the elements. New products were not, in a term that has become fashionable in recent years, biodegradable. The whole earth, it seemed, was becoming engulfed in its own trash. In the United States, the new energies came to a head on 22 April 1970 in the guise of Earth Day – a rash of demonstrations, teach-ins and other consciousness-raising events across the nation's schools and universities. Pushed forward by grassroots activism, the new movement bore little resemblance to older conservation, formulated and administered by central government and its bureaucratic structures.

An additional strand in environmental thinking, which sometimes sat uneasily with anxieties about pollution, focused on population growth. Paul Ehrlich, a Stanford University biologist and founder of the lobby Zero Population Growth, was firmly Malthusian in his emphasis on human capacities to outstrip finite natural resources. His concerns extended environmentalism decisively into the developing world.

Perhaps the most melodramatic expression of this calamitous thinking was the cover of his bestseller, *The Population Bomb* (1968), which depicted a cheerful baby set within a bubble topped by a lighted fuse – fitting accompaniment to his ominous opening statement: 'The battle to feed all of humanity is over.' The term 'population bomb', as Ehrlich noted, had been around since 1954 – his book's title was taken from a relatively unnoticed pamphlet of the same name. But at that time, in the absence of sufficient tinder, the idea had failed to ignite the same emotions.

Though the baby on the cover of Ehrlich's book was white, the writer was not so alarmist over US population growth of some 70 million between 1940 and 1970 – an increase of over 50 per cent. Ehrlich (who billed himself as a one-child parent and vasectomized) had in his sights the even more spectacular growth rates in the developing world, which census rates were showing as reaching 3 per cent per annum. The India he experienced in Delhi's teeming streets riveted his attention on people rather than pollution as the most pressing threat. Over-population as an idea had informed British colonial thinking in Africa and slipped easily into American discussions of overseas aid programmes. By 1970, debates about global environmental priorities were already beginning to polarize into the simplistic dichotomies of quantity of people versus quantity of consumption and pollution.

Commoner, a forerunner of 'social justice' environmentalism, emphasized first world consumption levels as more urgent than third world population growth. In a hypothetical scenario in which he evoked the 'eco-catastrophe' facing the world unless drastic measures were taken, Ehrlich credited the Indian ambassador to the United Nations with a powerful speech in which he pointed out that one American family dog placed a heavier burden on the world's supply of nutrition and energy than twenty-five average Indians (Ehrlich, 1970: 171–2). Commoner believed that economic development would solve the impending population crisis and that the obsession with third world numbers distracted attention from the real issue – maldistribution of wealth.[3] These views were in accordance with established theories of demographic transition, where rising wealth and urbanization signalled a decisive slowing in rates of population growth. Media coverage of the United Nations conference on population in Cairo, 1994, suggests that debate still gravitates to these positions.

The influx of these new ideas and concerns by no means drowned all established conservationist priorities. Growing affluence, leisure time and education widened the clientele for ideas and pursuits once the preserve of an élite. Americans could now afford both nature protection and economic development. The ardour for wild places, treasured not least for their recreational value, brought environmentalism up bluntly against dams and the concept of multipurpose river basin development. Located at the core of inherited conservation ideology, these notions embraced government control, job creation, energy provision, navigation, and – especially for American New Dealers – alleviation of rural poverty. A hallmark of the new, large-scale interest in John Muir's aesthetic ethos was the rejection of this type of conservation in the 1950s and 1960s – notably a project that would have backed up dam water into the hallowed Grand Canyon itself. Objections of an ecological nature reinforced aesthetic arguments. Land irrigated from dams can grow increasingly saline, actually killing the soil.

North American and western European popular environmentalism is arguably a full stomach phenomenon, of particular appeal to the middle classes. A central aspect of modern consumer society, whether in Houghton, Johannesburg, or Hollywood, Los Angeles, is the consumption of nature as part of the good life. It grows out of the territorial aggrandizement of the paraphernalia of modernity, most visible in suburbs, cars, roads, parking lots and shopping malls – along with increasingly artificial living environments, epitomized by air-conditioning. Uneasy coalitions across the class divide were possible in the US between environmentalists and labour to protest against use of pesticides in vineyards, but the influential wildlife and nature protection agenda did not speak to the priorities of blue-collar and non-white America.

Despite the limits to their appeal, western environmental ideas and language rapidly became internationalized. They were advanced by a new and diverse crop of international activist organizations such as the International Union for the Conservation of Nature and Natural Resources (1956), World Wildlife Fund (1961), Friends of the Earth (1969) and Greenpeace (1971). This global reach was manifest in UNESCO's idea of the world heritage site (1973). Africa's and America's wild places and creatures were humanity's heritage. More 'elefriends' could be spotted in London and New York City than among the rural Africans who lived much closer to them.

RACE, ENVIRONMENTALISM AND SOCIAL INEQUALITY

At this juncture, any profitable comparison between the United States and South Africa may appear to be short-circuited by the stark differences between an affluent nation with a large middle class and comfortable white majority, and one with an overwhelming preponderance of impoverished blacks where the new environmentalism had hardly penetrated. Yet if the United States had generated fresh green ideas it was by no means a stranger to the environmental problems associated with extensive poverty. Nor is South Africa immune from first world problems of consumption and pollution. Non-white 'minorities' already constitute a quarter of the US population and will form a majority early next century, at least in some regions, notably California and the southwest in general. Moreover, Native Americans represent a demographic majority over one third of US territory if Alaska is included. A growing disparity between haves and have-nots, to some extent congruent with colour, has been a feature of both South Africa and the United States.

In South Africa, opposition to the older resource-based conservation policies did not originate initially from American-derived 1960s environmentalism with its accent on amenity and 'rights of nature'. Rather it was expressed in black popular movements opposing government conservationist measures in the African reserve areas. Betterment and rehabilitation schemes (see chapter 4) cut across African patterns of settlement and farming and it was social disturbance that provoked protest. Africans admonished interfering officials not only with economic and technical arguments but also with snippets of folk wisdom, sometimes expressing their views in metaphors of ancestral respect.

Looking beyond indigenous ideas of non-literate communities, recent writers have tried to unearth a longer history of black intellectual concern about environmental decay. The African Farmers Union, led by D.D.T. Jabavu, has been offered as one interwar organization which tried to connect degradation in the homelands with the broader policy of segregation (Khan, forthcoming). They argued trenchantly that Africans required more land if they were to break the spiral of decline. However, Jabavu's conception of improvement, sparked by a formative visit to Alabama's Tuskegee Institute, envisaged a transformation of peasant agriculture, much along the technocratic lines being advocated by white officials (see chapter 4).

In the post-war decades, before the formulation of a new popular environmentalism, it was difficult for African nationalists and political leaders to incorporate the views of rural people defending old practices and local knowledge. The nationalist programme for the future was a modernizing one, geared to the achievement of civil rights, economic advance, and political power. Black thinkers during this period made limited progress in absorbing and reformulating conservation ideas so that they could speak to a popular constituency. As a result, black opinion tended to reject most conservation as 'authoritarian' policies, part of the apartheid system inflicted by the white minority (Ramphele, 1991: 13).

South African rural environmental problems have been bound up with the interconnected phenomena of poverty and rapid population growth. In 1904, there were less than 4 million Africans in total; by 1991 nearly 30 million. After the 1910s, the African reserves of South Africa were consolidated at about 13 per cent of the country. Until 1960 less than 40 per cent of the African population lived within them. Intensive controls over freedom of movement during the high apartheid years contributed to a banking up of African population in these reserves so that the numbers within homeland boundaries increased from 4 to about 11 million between 1960 and 1980.[4]

Areas which had been diagnosed as ecologically tarnished in the interwar years became even more heavily worn. The betterment system through which rural people were sucked into villages threw up as many environmental problems as it solved. Stocks of cattle and goats were supposed to be left in fenced pastures but these seldom remained intact for long. The result was that animals, instead of being brought home nightly to scattered homesteads, were now returned in greater numbers to villages which became new sites of erosion. In the absence of piped water, local sources often proved inadequate and became polluted. Firewood in the vicinity of these concentrated settlements was equally scarce (see below). Where large-scale population removals were superimposed on existing problems, land around new settlements became denuded bare earth.

The relationship between economic deprivation and environmental degradation, long evident in southern Africa, has become increasingly pronounced in the United States. Many of the nation's most deprived areas are also the most ecologically frail and abused. Despite advances toward civil equality and the emergence of a distinct black middle class, the subordinate socio-economic status of the bulk of Afro-Americans has altered little since the civil rights victories of the 1950s and 1960s. The non-white underclass inhabits 'fourth' world zones, physically if not legally segregated. The social and economic profile of Indian reservations in the rural West, or black rural communities in the South, is not dissimilar from homeland areas in South Africa. African townships in the apartheid era, though uniquely cordoned off on the urban peripheries, also stand comparison with black ghettos in the US urban north.

Toward the end of last century, the Native American was characterized as the 'vanishing' American, but the Indian population has been growing at a faster rate than the rest of the American population ever since this low point. The population of the Pine Ridge reservation in South Dakota doubled between 1960 and 1980 and the national total stands at over 1 million. This population rise has been accompanied by a further shrinking of their reserved land base. Some reservation land retained by treaty was divided into individual plots in a bid to turn Indians into smallholding farmers and the 'surplus' reverted to the public domain and eventually found its way into private hands. Other reservation lands were drowned by dam projects.

Today, reservations amount to only 4 per cent of the territory of the US, including Alaska, hemmed in by various federal conservation units as well as by private lands. High unemployment peaks at 85 per cent on the Lakota Sioux's Pine Ridge reservation. Pine Ridge is set in the nation's poorest county (three out of the ten poorest US counties overlap with Indian reservations) and within the shadow of Mount Rushmore, the nation's official 'shrine to democracy'. Life expectancy and infant mortality rates are much lower and higher respectively than the national average. Running water is virtually nonexistent on reservations, whose inhabitants travel considerable distances in pick-up trucks to haul supplies from irrigation ditches, stock ponds and other potentially contaminated sources.

The semi-autonomous status of American Indian reservations meant they were exempt from state laws, such as prohibitions on gambling, but not least environmental codes. Moreover, the spate of federal environmental legislation in the late 1960s and early 1970s left Indian lands unprotected and the federal Environmental Protection Agency with no jurisdiction. Physically displaced Native Americans sought work as miners, cowboys, farmers, and railroad construction crews, living in rural ghettos on the fringes of Euro-American society and settlements – just as the great majority of homeland-based Africans found employment as migrant workers in the mines and cities. The federal government's assimilationist relocation programmes encouraged this trend, and 50 per cent of the American Indian population is now urban.

Yet many established a pattern of seasonal return to remnant hunting, fishing and gathering grounds not only to supplement income but also to meet cultural needs. But access is circumscribed; those wildlife refuges and national forests carved out of Indian lands now serve largely as hunting grounds for white urban sportsmen, squeezing out Indian subsistence activities such as wild rice and maple syrup harvesting and medicinal plant cultivation. In South Africa, despite the pressures on resources in the African homelands, smallholder peasant cultivation has by no means collapsed and at least some see this as a viable part of their future. Similarly, not all American Indians regard higher employment levels – which essentially mean wage work in corporate, extractive industries – as the way forward.

Struggles over the control of natural resources in rural South Africa occasionally verged on rebellion. The best-known episode was the Pondoland revolt of 1960. One of the main issues at stake was government attempts to reserve coastal forests, for aesthetic and ecological reasons, in which rural people were accustomed to gather wood, find medicinal ingredients and hunt small game. Confrontations over access to the forests were exacerbated by the threats of villagization and betterment. Chiefs who sympathized with the government had their homesteads burned and a few were killed. It took an invasion with armoured divisions and helicopters to restore control over the region.

American Indians (citizens and voters since 1924) did not have a formal system of apartheid around which protest could crystallize. But the 'red power' movement of the 1960s coalesced around efforts to regain control over natural resources – as was sometimes the case in rural South Africa. Throughout the nation, Indians clashed with state-level fish and game authorities as they reasserted their ancestral right to hunt and fish both on and off reservation without licences and in any season in order to feed themselves. Nineteenth-century federal treaty provisions guaranteeing fishing rights in their 'usual and accustomed grounds' – many of which were off reservation – had been largely abrogated. Indians saw this as kowtowing to the interests of white sports and commercial fishers, though the need to conserve breeding stocks was usually cited in justification. The state of Washington, Janet McCloud of the Tulalip tribe declared, 'must think that the steelhead [trout] swam over behind the Mayflower' (Steiner, 1968: 55).

Civil disobedience in the Pacific Northwest took the form of a series of fish-ins and subsequent jailings that secured a high media profile, with Marlon Brando, for example, casting a net into the disputed waters. Indians occupied Alcatraz Island in San Francisco Bay, site of an abandoned federal penitentiary, for over a year (1969–70), arguing that the island resembled a typical Indian reservation because, among other things, 'the soil is rocky and non-productive; and the land does not support game'. The protestors spoke of establishing a centre for Native American ecological studies on the island: 'We will work to de-pollute the air and waters of the Bay Area . . . restore fish and animal life' (Zinn, 1980: 516, 518). Indian fishing and hunting rights were eventually upheld by the Supreme Court (1979) but the restoration of ancestral lands is a far more difficult proposition since the bulk have passed into private ownership.[5]

Restoration of those pieces that remain federally owned – parks, refuges and forests – is at least feasible, though likely to be fiercely resisted by the conservation agencies involved (Gordon-McCutchan, 1991). Some environmentalists, while perhaps sympathetic to the romantic idea of an eco-friendly Indian heritage, are just as apprehensive about the deregulation these restorations might entail. They draw evidence from the multiplication of gambling joints and their associated 'vices' on the reservations. Strikingly, casinos – illegal in the old white South Africa – also spread in the South African black homelands, spawned by Sol Kerzner's Sun chain. Sun City, in the former Bophuthatswana, rivals the giant Foxwoods, in the Mashantucket Pequot Indian reservation in Connecticut. Native American spokespeople are divided between, on the one hand, asserting their rights to develop their lands and, on the other, calming such fears. The latter view involves assurances that the restoration of federal forest, park and refuge lands to Native ownership would simply transfer management rather than abolish categories of protection (LaDuke, 1992).

While apartheid was entrenched, and the government was committed to consolidating the African homelands as independent states, Africans could only stake claims to lands through this system. The gradual unravelling of white rule over the last few years has created new opportunities for land reform. Some privately owned black farms, commandeered by the state in earlier decades because they were in 'white' farmlands, have already been returned to black ownership. Beyond a modest restitution of such lands, a broader redistribution programme raises acute conservation as well as political difficulties. First, the country's demography is different from the USA, Canada or Australia where native land claims have been entertained. If, for example, a 'Zulu' tribal right to land were recognized, millions of landless people could qualify – an outcome which would extend existing environmental stresses in black rural areas. The ANC government has in any case steered clear of encouraging such politically divisive ethnic land claims. Second, where black communal purchases are made, the capacity of the government to regulate new forms of occupation is restricted.

Indian reservations, like national parks to a degree, represented cast-off lands considered worthless in terms of natural resources, especially farmable lands. The valueless, however, has been revalued in terms of mineral potential. Mining throughout the West experienced a boom during World War Two and after: zeolite (clay), oil, coal and, particularly in the 1950s, uranium. American business began showing interest in profit-maximizing stripmining of Indian-owned minerals in the late 1960s – an interest that quickened during the energy shortages of the 1970s and which tribal councils, dominated by the development-minded, authorized in return for slender royalties and a few jobs. More recently, Indian lands have also been attracting attention for their potential in the storage of municipal garbage, medical and radioactive waste (Knox, 1993).

Meanwhile, reservations suffer from inadequate supplies of fuel-wood, electricity and water yet bear the brunt of pollution from nearby processing plants. The resonant South African image of black women carrying unwieldy loads of fuelwood passing under power cables has its compelling, if less familiar counterpart in the high-tension cables that span the Navajo reservation, down which juice from the Four Corners coal-fired power plant and Glen Canyon Dam surges to southern Californian cities and pulsating Las Vegas neon. One third of all low sulphur coal and two thirds of uranium mined in the US are on reservation lands. Cancer incidence and birth defects on reservations where uranium has been mined are much higher than the national average.

South Africa shares many of the environmental problems associated with mining in the northern hemisphere. Much of the country's energy is derived from cheap and abundant low grade coal. Massive quantities, over 50 per cent of domestic consumption, are burnt to produce electricity, especially in the Transvaal, to feed the largest urban concentration in the country as well as the hungriest industries. In recognition of its lack of domestic oil reserves and in response to the threat of embargos, the South African government funded the world's largest oil from coal processing plants, into which 20 per cent of national coal production was funnelled by the early 1980s. In the absence of electricity and fuelwood supplies, coal is the main source of household fuel in the biggest African townships such as Soweto. The resulting sulphur and nitrogen oxide emissions produce high levels of pollution in the southern and eastern Transvaal. Johannesburg's smog rivals that of the industrial heartlands of Europe and America.

Prior to the New Deal of the 1930s, nine out of ten American farms were still geared to horse and hand power and had no piped water, while three quarters fetched their water from creeks and heated their homes with wood stoves. Coal and electricity increasingly displaced woodfuel, and United Nations figures for 1978 show North America as a whole using less than one-sixteenth the amount of wood used for fuel in Africa (Simmons, 1989: 301). In the rural areas of southern Africa, where coal is hard to come by, a large proportion of Africans still do not have access to electricity and are dependent on wood, collected by women and transported on their heads. In Lesotho, where natural wood is rare, peat-like dried dung is burned instead. This practice brings to mind the burning of buffalo chips (*bois de vache*) by Indians and the first white travellers and settlers on the American Great Plains, now but a hazy, if pungent, memory that lingers mainly in stories of Laura Ingalls Wilder. The use of manure for fuel deprives the soil of badly needed nutrients, presenting a hard choice between fuel or fertilizer. The demand for wood around black settlements not only denudes the vegetation but, as this resource becomes more scarce, the labour time of women in daily collection rapidly increases. Heavy head loads carried ever further can, in addition, lead to spinal problems.

Large forestry schemes, though they may satisfy the industrial demand from newsprint to nappies, have little impact on these immediate needs. Three main routes have been suggested to solve the rural fuelwood crisis in Africa. Some authors focus on maximizing fuel use by trying to improve upon the open fires set under three-legged iron pots which is the most common rural kitchen scenario. Following, as it were, in Ben Franklin's footsteps, they focus on enhancing the efficiency of stoves. Second, Munslow (1988) argues for a redirection of afforestation strategies (see chapter 3). Foresters, he suggests, cannot see the trees for the forests. Priority should rather be given to decentralized agroforestry by incorporating a wide variety of trees into smallholder farming systems. This approach promises environmental benefits by supplementing monocultural uniformity with a range of complementary indigenous trees – a soft path that taps local knowledge and experience.

Third, there is sufficient generating capacity in South Africa to electrify rural homesteads if only the costs of the network can be met. Rural electrification appeals to many as the single most environmentally friendly measure the new South African government could take, also liberating women in particular from drudgery. The cost, however, will be counted in yet more sulphur-spewing smoke stacks. Moreover, as in rural Appalachia, wired up by the Tennessee Valley Authority during the 1930s, electricity may snap the vestiges of old styles of life distinctive for their close dependence on the natural world.

Environmental poverty has health as well as economic consequences. In the early decades of this century, white medical men blamed widespread rural tuberculosis among Africans partly on the lung-choking smoke of wood fires in badly ventilated huts. A more likely cause was mal- or undernutrition and the infectious milieu of the mining compounds, factors which have contributed to persistently high rates of tuberculosis to the present day. Urban squalor, together with AIDS, has fuelled a similar upsurge in major American cities. Poor city dwellers also suffer a high and debilitating exposure to pollutants, such as lead and dioxins. Black American activists have documented the disproportionate siting of toxic waste dumps in their communities. Houston, Texas has been locating its solid waste sites in Afro-American neighbourhoods since the 1920s. African locations had been juxtaposed to sewerage works in more than one South African city.

Environmental historians are being urged to introduce the categories of gender, class and ethnicity more seriously into their analytical framework, and to correct their bias toward the non-urban, non-industrial environment. Similarly, environmentalists of both regions are under pressure to move beyond their white concerns and old constituencies. Those seeking to build bi-racial reform coalitions modelled on the early 1960s American civil rights movement, and to empower local communities, insist that socio-economic justice must become one of the central objectives of urban, 'backyard' environmentalism (*Sierra*, 1993; Merchant, 1992: 162, 164–7 and 192–3; Gottlieb, 1993b). The goals of social justice are forcing a redefinition of environmentalism's familiar parameters. In the USA, 'blue-collar' activists, many of them women and non-white, are working in the urban context for the greening of the concrete jungle whose natural features are largely restricted to the indomitable weeds that sprout in pavement cracks and on abandoned lots. They urge that opportunities, provided partly by deindustrialization of city centres, be taken by converting wasteland into parks, productive gardens and city farms, as well as by developing energy-efficient public housing and mass transit schemes.

The tightening of environmental regulations – particularly pollution controls – in richer countries can have negative repercussions for the developing world. Though its use was banned in the US in 1972, DDT continued to be manufactured there and sold to less protected regions. Economically marginal and politically impotent communities with low wage demands and weak environmental rules are also exposed to the 'garbage imperialism' of the toxic waste industry. Thor Chemicals built the world's largest mercury recycling plant on the borders of KwaZulu. The import of toxic wastes to this plant, some of it controlled by US multinational American Cyanamid, mobilized an alliance in 1990 of unionized chemical workers, environmentalists (Earthlife Africa and Greenpeace), African peasants and white commercial farmers. Parallel protests confronted Cyanamid's Bound Brook plant in the United States (Cock and Koch, 1991: 25–6, 82–3). The waste merchants target homelands, making tempting financial offers. The 'Black Caucus' in the US Congress is sponsoring a bill to ban their country's exports to the KwaZulu/Natal plant.

Corporations repelled from other American states since the 1960s by stricter environmental controls and enforcement have received a warm welcome in the South in the shape of tax exemption offers for their LULUs (locally unwanted land uses): factories, paper mills, hazardous waste incinerators, waste dumps and landfills. As a result, southern air and water are the dirtiest in the nation (Schueler, 1992). One distinctive feature of the events marking the twentieth anniversary of Earth Day in 1990 was Jesse Jackson's 'toxic tour' of afflicted Afro-American communities.

Minority group campaigners against pollution accuse mainstream US environmental organizations of obsession with 'élitist' goals such as wilderness preservation. A similar chasm has opened up in South Africa recently as radical activists influenced by the American environmental justice movement have rediscovered ecological issues – for so long disparaged as a part of the strategy of colonial hegemony. A broad-based movement turning on labour rights rather than established conservation elements has highlighted the workplace as an environment. Industrial health experts and radical lawyers have worked over the last decade with the powerful new independent black trade union movements to publicize the dangers of asbestos dust and herbicides. A proliferation of small community environmental groups has broadened these workplace issues into demands for basic services such as clean water. Their approach is captured in a popular magazine, *New Ground*. More established conservation societies have been obliged to respond to this more 'people-centred' orientation by the rapidity of political change (Khan, 1994).

For all its grassroots impetus, the new environmentalism became as dependent on an interventionist state as the old conservation. The cornerstone of US federal legislation – the National Environmental Policy Act of 1969 – commanded sufficient national momentum to be passed under Nixon's Republican presidency. This introduced the environmental impact statement into federal decision-making and set up the executive-branch Environmental Protection Agency (1970) to co-ordinate pollution control and rap the knuckles of corporate offenders. With 13,000 employees and a budget of $5.6 billion by 1980, the EPA was the largest regulatory body within the federal government. Lacking a boisterous middle-class movement, South Africa has no equivalent, popularly inspired legislation. However, a formidable array of Acts generated not least within the large state bureaucracy has been developed with the potential to control both agriculture and industry.

A far-reaching general Environment Conservation Act was passed in 1982, supplemented by the Conservation of Agricultural Resources Act (1983) which consolidated a host of earlier soil conservation measures. Under the latter legislation, it is not even possible for a farmer on private land to break fresh ground for crops without notifying local officials. Drought relief assistance for farmers in the early 1990s became dependent on meeting government-imposed limits on stock numbers. Similarly, American farmers became ineligible for US Department of Agriculture crop support and insurance programmes in the mid-1980s if they brought land designated as erosive into production.

Radical environmentalism in South Africa is firmly part of a broader socio-economic and political critique, an anthropocentric approach with the interests of the less privileged at its heart. Radical environmentalism in the US, by contrast, has tended to be more biocentric, championing the vulnerable and violated members of the natural community. At its most vehement, this deep ecological viewpoint insists on the intrinsic rights of natural species and places, regardless of their economic, aesthetic or recreational value (Naess, 1972; Devall and Sessions, 1985; Nash, 1989). While the spotted owl of the Pacific Northwest and its old growth forest is the rallying hoot for those who put the earth first, the human right to clean water drives an environmentalism of social justice. Perhaps the human constituency for the owl and the elephant will be more powerful when these basic human requirements have been met – assuming there are still owls and elephants around by then.

POSTSCRIPT: TAMING THE WILD

We have sought to write an environmental history rather than an environmentalist's history. This has entailed an attempt to examine the interrelation of ecological and economic/cultural change. Rather than espouse a 'great tradition' of environmental thought we have sought to examine how and why different and sometimes conflicting positions on environmental loss and nature's redemption emerged. A pivotal element in such understandings is the timespan within which processes of change are assessed. A single generation's irredeemable loss in topsoil or indigenous forest may appear far less cataclysmic across centuries of change or even paltry on a geological or climatic scale. So we have dealt in transformations as well as destructions. The pace of change has quickened and apocalyptic outcomes cannot be ruled out. But trees rise as well as fall, even if new growth does not replicate old. An investigation of longer-term transformations can be enhanced by a wide geographical coverage of disparate regions, which allows for the discovery of contrasting outcomes.

It is no challenge to enumerate points of divergence between the United States and South Africa. Aside from geophysical distinctiveness turning on elements such as size, soil and climate, the United States is bigger, has more people and was founded on a settler majority. At a far earlier stage than South Africa, a democratic political culture evolved which, while allowing for racial subordination, nevertheless permitted far broader political participation and organization. In consequence, environmental policy has been the subject of intense disputation, as interest groups mobilized to advance their causes and exploit the system of checks and balances. Ironically, democracy has not always been conducive to protectionist initiatives, relying as they do on government intervention. In the racially exclusive political system established in South Africa, by contrast, civil society was more restricted and the state enjoyed greater powers over policy formulation and implementation. At the same time, we have sought to highlight what remain illuminating convergences in both experiences and interpretation. The common ground in terms of variety of climate, indigenous practices and introduced economic and social systems has provided a sound basis for comparative musings. It would have been less productive to have coupled South Africa with Thailand, or the United States with Nigeria.

The expansion of Europe and the communities this established in southern Africa and North America inaugurated far-reaching sequences of change in the ecology of the colonized continents. The capitalist systems that came to dictate human relations with nature were often geared to the gobbling of resources for maximum short-term profit, a veritable *raubwirtschaft* (predatory economy).[6] Entrepreneurs and private owners made the proverbial fast buck[7] by shooting out deer, overstocking with cattle, ploughing for four or five bumper wheat harvests, or gouging out gold for as long as international price levels were right. Yet within these transformative tendencies resided capacities for containment. The propensities of capitalism have proved unpredictable and can in certain cases work to the benefit of its former victims.

Buffalo, and buffalo grasses, are being restored to the American plains and springbok (together with rooigras) are returning to the Karoo and neighbouring grasslands – two regions whose abuse provides striking examples of the tragedy of unrestrained private control and the denaturing of the wild. Celebrity ranchers such as actress Jane Fonda and CNN mogul Ted Turner are stocking their recently acquired Montanan spread near Bozeman with Plains fauna. Adventure novelist Wilbur Smith, author of bloodthirsty hunting sagas such as *A Time to Die* (1989), has bought a number of Karoo farms in South Africa with the intention of expunging the exotic if unremarkable sheep and restoring wildlife to them; one of his latest bestsellers, *Elephant Song* (1991), pursues a born-again, empathetic conservationism 'against the forces of evil, greed and corruption' (jacket blurb). These restorationist enthusiasms, together with some extension of national parklands and their restocking, have resulted in a marked growth in buffalo, kudu and springbok numbers since the mid-1980s. But the return of the native to the Karoo and the Plains coincides with the latest agrarian crisis. The post-Dust-Bowl revival of farming fortunes had been achieved through technological fixes rather than by more cautious farming practices (see chapter 4). Aquifers which have accumulated over millenia are being depleted far more rapidly than the water is being replaced by rainfall. Falling prices for grain and beef, declining land values, weakening government subsidies and rising costs for fertilizer, fuel and water extraction signal that cropping and ranching are decreasingly viable in a volatile environment. Wool prices have been low and interest rates high for South African sheep and cattle farmers through the 1980s, pushing them to explore alternative land-use schemes.

Robert Scott, a researcher at the Institute of the Rockies, recommends that about a tenth of the state of Montana be converted into an African-style game reserve known as the 'Big Open' where buffalo, deer, elk and antelope can sport instead. Richard Cowling, a South African botanist, has with less fanfare suggested the recommunalization of the Karoo so that it could be peopled by nomads and wildlife again. The vision of an eco-tourist and sports hunting economy – an American Serengeti – shooting up among abandoned farms and towns as a sustainable alternative to the traditional capitalist boom and bust cycle is particularly associated with Deborah and Frank Popper. Leading protagonists of the 'Buffalo Commons' notion, the Poppers 'foresee safaris across Kansas'. Some ranchers are already hosting lucrative hunting safaris in line with their South African counterparts (1989: 110, 112; Cowling, 1991).

A wholesale re-establishment of the buffalo or springbok commons would require massive government purchase of marginal or played-out private holdings as envisaged by the more ambitious New Dealers but whose implementation in the 1930s was restricted to the creation of a few million acres of grasslands. The more feasible route of private game ranching, well established in southern Africa, is increasingly winning American converts. Habits are changing for sound ecological and economic reasons. Buffalo can survive drought and blizzard and crop the often thin grasses more gently but also more efficiently than cattle. They are equipped to excavate through up to five feet of snow to reach grass (cattle use their noses instead of their hoofs) and to defend their calves against the ravages of spring storms by forming a corral of adult bodies.

The advantages do not work for all farmers. While game farming is popular in the Transvaal where there is browse as well as grass, landowners in the colder highveld grasslands find the natural vegetation insufficiently diverse for profitable game raising given that beef markets remain buoyant. Many American ranchers also appear less flexible. According to one defiant South Dakota stockman, hostile to what locals call 'Californication' (meaning not the spread of suburbs and shopping malls but an environmentalist agenda): 'It doesn't matter if the towns get smaller, or disappear, it doesn't matter if there is just one goddamned farmer left – that man will be raising beef at a price the American family wants to pay' (*The Sunday Telegraph Magazine*, 6 June 1992: 53). But the hegemony of beef is not unassailable. Buffalo ranchers (who now number around 1,000) are stretched to keep up with the demand for tasty, low-cholesterol buffalo steaks from as far away as Belgium. South African buck meat was reputedly sold as East European venison to gain access to international markets during the years of sanctions. The revival of a market for game products, uncannily reminiscent of nineteenth-century trends which threatened their extinction, might yet ensure the multiplication of these animals.

Rather like a non-governmental version of Operation Campfire in Zimbabwe, buffalo ranching is proving especially attractive to Native Americans eager to revitalize moribund reservation economies and reconnect with past culture. As fences are taken down, land pooled and the range stocked with communally owned buffalo (*tatanka*), Native Americans have the chance to recall the wild and revive the good husbandry which they associate with aboriginal peoples and the idea of the commons.

Yet even here increasing numbers of buffalo do not constitute wildness regained. They may be free-range but they remain farm stock. Appropriately, the herd of buffalo that starred in Kevin Costner's movie paean to the untamed in man and nature, *Dances with Wolves*, were 'domestic' buffalo filmed on a ranch in South Dakota. The taste of renatured wild has more than a hint of tameness.

NOTES

1 Grassroots is an American political term dating from the turn-of-the-century Progressive era, which became popular in South Africa in the highly politicized 1970s and 1980s.
2 This was a reference to the alleged role of Harriet Beecher Stowe's heartrending novel in alerting northern public consciousness to the evils of slavery in the antebellum South.

3 Ehrlich did become increasingly sympathetic to the stress on economic development in the third world and restraint on western consumption levels as the way to deal with population problems in a world of finite resources (Ehrlich, 1971: 79–80).

4 Reserved areas for Africans date back to the nineteenth century and were formalized and extended in legislation of 1913 and 1936. The extended reserves became a lynchpin of apartheid policy after 1948 and the Afrikaner Nationalist government renamed them homelands. The intention was that they would become the basis for the balkanization of the country.

5 Some patches were returned under the Indian Claims Commission that operated between the 1940s and 1970s but most restitution has consisted of financial compensation. Alaska is the great exception.

6 The term was popularized by the German economic geographer, Ernst Friedrich, in 1904.

7 This colloquialism for the dollar derives, appropriately, from the skin trade. An adult deer hide fetched one Spanish dollar.

REFERENCES AND FURTHER READING

Abbey, Edward (1977) 'The second rape of the West', in *The Journey Home: Some Words in Defense of the American West*, New York: Dutton.

Brimblecombe, Peter (1987) *The Big Smoke: A History of Air Pollution in London since Medieval Times*, London: Methuen.

Bullard, Robert D. (1990) *Dumping in Dixie: Race, Class and Environmental Quality*, Boulder: Westview Press.

Carson, Rachel (1962) *Silent Spring*, Boston: Houghton Mifflin.

Coates, Peter (1989a) 'Project Chariot: Alaskan roots of environmentalism', *Alaska History*, 4 (2) (Fall), 1–31.

——— (1989b) 'Support your right to arm bears (and peccadillos): The higher ground and further shores of American environmentalism', *Journal of American Studies*, 23 (3) (December), 439–46.

——— (1993a) *The Trans-Alaska Pipeline Controversy: Technology, Conservation and the Frontier*, Fairbanks: University of Alaska Press.

——— (1993b) *In Nature's Defence: Americans and Conservation*, Keele: Keele University Press/British Association for American Studies.

Cock, Jacklyn and Koch, Eddie (eds) (1991) *Going Green: People, Politics and the Environment in South Africa*, Cape Town: Oxford University Press.

Commoner, Barry (1971) *The Closing Circle: Confronting the Environmental Crisis*, London: Cape.

Cowling, R. (1991) 'Options for rural land use in southern Africa: An ecological perspective', in M. de Klerk (ed.), *A Harvest of Discontent: The Land Question in South Africa*, Cape Town: Institute for a Democratic Alternative in South Africa.

Devall, Bill and Sessions, George (1985) *Deep Ecology*, Salt Lake City: Peregrine Smith.

Dunlap, Thomas R. (1981) *DDT: Scientists, Citizens and Public Policy*, Princeton: Princeton University Press.

Durning, Alan B. (1990) *Apartheid's Environmental Toll*, Worldwatch Paper 95 (May).

Ehrlich, Paul (1968) *The Population Bomb*, New York: Ballantines/Friends of the Earth.

—— (1970) 'Eco-Catastrophe!' in *The Environmental Handbook*, New York: Ballantines/Friends of the Earth.

—— (1971) *Playboy* Interview in *Project Survival*, Chicago: Playboy Press.

Fleming, Donald (1972) 'Roots of the new conservation movement', *Perspectives in American History*, 6, 7–91.

Fox, Stephen J. (1985) *The American Conservation Movement: John Muir and His Legacy*, Madison: University of Wisconsin Press.

Fuggle, R. and Rabie, A. (eds) (1992) *Environmental Management in South Africa*, Cape Town: Juta.

Glacken, C. (1967) *Traces on the Rhodian Shore*, Berkeley: University of California Press.

Gordon-McCutchan, R.C. (1991) *The Taos Indians and the Battle for Blue Lake*, Santa Fe: Red Crane Books.

Gottlieb, Robert (1993a) 'Reconstructing environmentalism: Complex movements, diverse roots', *Environmental History Review*, 17 (4) (Winter), 1–19.

—— (1993b) *Forcing the Spring: The Transformation of the American Environmental Movement*, Washington, D.C.: Island Press.

Graham, Frank (1970) *Since Silent Spring*, Boston: Houghton Mifflin.

Hays, Samuel P. (1987) *Beauty, Health and Permanence: Environmental Politics in the United States, 1955–1985*, Cambridge: Cambridge University Press.

Huntley, B., Siegfried, R. and Sunter, C. (1989) *South African Environments into the 21st Century*, Cape Town: Tafelberg.

Khan, Farieda (1994) 'Environmentalism in a changing South Africa', unpublished paper presented at *Journal of Southern African Studies* conference, University of York.

—— (forthcoming) 'Rewriting South Africa's environmental history: The role of the Native Farmers' Association', *Journal of Southern African Studies*, 20 (4).

Knox, Margaret L. (1993) 'Their mothers' keepers', *Sierra*, 78 (March/April), 50–7, 81–4.

LaDuke, Winona (1992) 'Indigenous environmental perspectives: A North American primer', *Akwe:kon Journal* (Summer), 52–71.

Lear, Linda (1993) 'Rachel Carson's *Silent Spring*', *Environmental History Review*, 17 (2) (Summer), 23–48.

Lutts, Ralph (1985) 'Chemical fallout: Rachel Carson's *Silent Spring*, radioactive fallout, and the environmental movement', *Environmental Review*, 9 (Fall), 211–25.

McAllister, P. A. (1989) 'Resistance to "Betterment" in the Transkei: A case study from Willowvale District', *Journal of Southern African Studies*, 15 (2), 346–68.

McGucken, William (1991) *Biodegradable: Detergents and the Environment*, College Station: Texas A&M University Press.

Mbeki, Govan (1964) *The Peasants' Revolt*, Harmondsworth: Penguin.

Melosi, Martin (ed.) (1980) *Pollution and Reform in American Cities, 1870–1930*, Austin: University of Texas Press.

—— (1981) *Garbage in the Cities: Refuse, Reform and the Environment, 1880–1980*, College Station: Texas A&M University Press.

—— (1993) 'The place of the city in environmental history', *Environmental History Review*, 17 (Spring), 1–23.

Merchant, Carolyn (1992) *Radical Ecology: The Search for a Livable World*, New York: Routledge.

Munslow, Barry (1988) *The Fuelwood Trap: A Study of the SADCC Region*, London: Earthscan.

Naess, Arne (1972) 'The shallow and the deep, long-range ecology movement', *Inquiry*, 16, 95–100.

Nash, Roderick (1982) 'The international perspective', (chapter 16) in *Wilderness and the American Mind*, New Haven: Yale University Press.

—— (1989) *The Rights of Nature: A History of Environmental Ethics*, Madison: University of Wisconsin Press.

Norwood, Vera (1993) *Made from This Earth: American Women and Nature*, Chapel Hill: University of North Carolina Press.

Oelschlaeger, Max (1991) *The Idea of Wilderness: From Prehistory to the Age of Ecology*, New Haven: Yale University Press.

Platzky, L. and Walker, C. (1985) *The Surplus People: Forced Removals in South Africa*, Johannesburg: Ravan Press.

Popper, Deborah and Popper, Frank (1989) 'The fate of the Plains', in Ed Marston (ed.), *Reopening the Western Frontier*, Washington, D.C.: Island Press.

Ramphele, M. (ed.) (1991) *Restoring the Land: Environment and Change in Post-Apartheid South Africa*, London: Panos.

Schueler, Donald G. (1992) 'Southern exposure', *Sierra*, 77 (November/December), 42–9, 76.

Sierra (1993) 'A place at the table: *Sierra* roundtable on race, justice, and the environment', 78 (May/June), 51–8, 90–1.

Simmons, I.G. (1989) *Changing the Face of the Earth: Environment, History, Culture*, Oxford: Blackwell.

Steiner, Stan (1968) *The New Indians*, New York: Delta.

Wilson, F. and Ramphele, M. (1989) *Uprooting Poverty: The South African Challenge*, Cape Town: David Philip.

Wylie, D. (1989) 'The changing face of hunger in southern Africa', *Past & Present*, 122, 159–99.

Zinn, Howard (1980) *A People's History of the United States*, London: Longman.

Index